The Sticky Learning Framework:
Adaptive Learning Models for Knowledge Absorption, Retention, and Application

By Peter Hollins,

Author and Researcher at

petehollins.com

Table of Contents

[INTRODUCTION](#)   5

CHAPTER 1: THE DEEP LEARNING MINDSET   11

THE POWER OF A GROWTH MINDSET IN ACHIEVING DEEP LEARNING   11
AUTOTELIC ACTIVITIES: THE GATEWAY TO DEEP LEARNING AND INNER GROWTH   24
METACOGNITION: THE KEY TO SMARTER, DEEPER LEARNING   37
DELIBERATE PRACTICE FOR DEEP LEARNING: QUALITY OVER QUANTITY   46

CHAPTER 2: WHAT TRUE LEARNING LOOKS LIKE   61

UNLOCKING DEEP LEARNING THROUGH VYGOTSKY'S ZONE OF PROXIMAL DEVELOPMENT   61
SPACED REPETITION: A SIMPLE PATH TO DEEP LEARNING   73
MIX IT UP AND SPREAD IT OUT: HOW INTERLEAVING BUILDS SMARTER, LONG-TERM LEARNING   81
TASK-SWITCHING: REFRESH FOCUS WITH COGNITIVE MICRO-BREAKS   90

CHAPTER 3: STAY IN THE GOLDILOCKS ZONE   99

PRACTICE FOCUSED ATTENTION BY FILTERING OUT IRRELEVANT INFORMATION   104
STRENGTHEN WORKING MEMORY WITH CHALLENGING COGNITIVE TASKS   106
IMPROVE IMPULSE CONTROL THROUGH FAST-PACED DECISION GAMES   107
COGNITIVE LOAD MANAGEMENT: LIGHTEN THE MENTAL LOAD TO UNLOCK DEEP LEARNING   109

BALANCING STRESS FOR BETTER LEARNING: WHAT THE YERKES-DODSON CURVE TEACHES US 120

CHAPTER 4: LEARNING IS A DIALOGUE 135

HOW ASKING THE RIGHT QUESTIONS FUELS DEEP LEARNING 135
PRE-TESTING AND QUIZZING YOURSELF: A SHORTCUT TO DEEP LEARNING 144
PREDICTION BEFORE INSTRUCTION: SPARK CURIOSITY TO BOOST RETENTION 152
CLARIFYING CONCEPTS BY TEACHING YOURSELF 162

CHAPTER 5: THE MANY LANGUAGES OF LEARNING 175

VOCABULARY INSTRUCTION AND DEEP LEARNING: UNLOCKING THE POWER OF WORDS 175
MULTIMODAL LEARNING: HOW IMAGES, WORDS AND MOVEMENT WORK TOGETHER TO SPARK DEEP UNDERSTANDING 184
THE POWER OF PERSPECTIVE—TAKING IN DEEP LEARNING 194

CHAPTER 6: WHAT MEMORIES ARE MADE OF 209

CONTEXT-DEPENDENT MEMORY: HOW MATCHING THE MOMENT DEEPENS YOUR LEARNING 209
EMOTION TAGGING: ENHANCE MEMORY WITH MINI STORIES 218
CONFLICT-BASED ENCODING: STRENGTHEN LEARNING BY CHALLENGING MISCONCEPTIONS 228

CONCLUSION 237

Introduction

"The capacity to learn is a gift; the ability to learn is a skill; the willingness to learn is a choice."

- **Brian Herbert**

What *is* learning?

An inborn ability?

An acquired skill?

A conscious decision?

According to author Brian Herbert, it's all three.

Imagine this: You pass from this world to the next and come to a grand chamber where you meet the ancient Egyptian god Anubis. He appears before you with a scale.

No, this is not the mythical "weighing of the heart" you may have heard about from ancient Egyptian mythology, but a *weighing of the mind*.

Your total consciousness is placed on the scales, and appraised.

What have you truly, genuinely learned during your time on this earth?

What difficult things do you understand now that eluded you previously?

What authentic insight have you gained?

In the deepest possible sense, what do you *know*?

This magical set of scales is not fooled by jargon, regurgitated second-hand soundbites, or automatic responses. Anubis isn't impressed by your formal qualifications or awards, and he doesn't care what books you have on your bookshelf. No, this mother of all exams measures the real thing only: the true depths of your knowledge, understanding, and wisdom.

So, how would *you* measure up?

Let's set these deep existential questions aside for a moment and zoom out.

In this book, we are not really making the distinction between **deep learning** and **shallow learning.**

Instead (keeping these mythical scales in mind) we want to distinguish between **learning,** and **the mere image or illusion of learning.**

The modern educational system, hustle culture, and the commercial self-help industry? They most often trade in *superficial, external markers* of learning—not learning itself. If you've picked up this book, it's likely that you already understand how limited and limiting this approach is.

The hope is that by the end of this book, you'll not only have a more sophisticated understanding of what *real* learning actually looks like, but you'll possess the mindset, habits, and practical tools to actually achieve it.

Few of us need to be reminded that the world is complex and growing more unpredictable by the day. The looming specter of Artificial Intelligence is forcing us to determine, in a hurry, what constitutes *human* intelligence.

While the world feverishly discusses the wonders of "machine learning", it's worth considering the nature of your own learning processes, and what they may yield beyond the machine-like or the superficial.

What are your goals?

- Learning an instrument
- Acquiring a new language
- Mastering a new set of occupational skills
- Improving academic understanding
- Cultivating better athletic performance
- Passing an important test
- Boosting your creative and problem-solving abilities
- Developing better life habits

- Broadening your horizons

Whether your aspirations are personal or professional, ambitious or modest, short-term or lifelong, this book can help you.

In the chapters that follow we will not be focusing exclusively on methods, approaches, or techniques. Instead, our book is built on a basic premise: *How* you do something is more important than *what* you do.

Knowing how to learn is the ultimate transferable skill.

If you have mastered the deep learning mindset, you'll never wonder, "Does this apply to my situation?" or "How can I make this work for my goals?" because you will have developed the very mindset that allows you to identify, cultivate, and apply the core principles to *every* learning situation.

In these chapters we will:

- Discover the exact **attitude, mindset, and core beliefs** that are most reliably associated with high performance—and why most of us get it wrong
- Explore how learning actually occurs, and how to maximize that process using **simple, evidence-based approaches**
- Understand why you slip, plateau, procrastinate, stall, or fall off the wagon

entirely—and easy ways to prevent it ever happening again (yes, really!)
- Find out why cramming, rote memorization, punishing schedules, and exhaustion just don't work (and what does)
- See how conventional learning techniques are letting you down and how you may already be using superior learning techniques without even knowing it
- Learn how to **create robust, lasting memories** that really stick—without force

All we need to begin is the willingness to make a decision: to choose internally to say to ourselves, "Yes, I'm ready to learn."

Are you ready to take that first step?

Deep learning is not about what you do, but how you think. Let's dig in and start laying that foundation.

Chapter 1: The Deep Learning Mindset

The Power of a Growth Mindset in Achieving Deep Learning

"No matter what your ability is, effort is what ignites that ability and turns it into accomplishment."

- **Carol Dweck**

In 2007, author and psychologist Carol Dweck published the bestselling book *Mindset: The New psychology of Success.* She wanted to answer a question you may have also asked: Why do some people succeed so phenomenally in life, even when other more intelligent and more talented people don't?

Dweck's research led her to a simple premise:

Success is not just about ability.

It's about how you *think* about ability.

Dweck found consistent patterns in the way her own students approached their learning.

In the attitudes they held.

In the beliefs that guided them.

- Some students saw intelligence and ability as unchangeable and innate. Just something you're born with. Dweck called this constellation of beliefs a **fixed mindset.**
- Other students saw intelligence and ability as things to be acquired and developed. Something you can work for, even if you don't have it to begin with. Dweck called this constellation of beliefs a **growth mindset.**

There is something very profound in Dweck's observations: The biggest determinant of our success with learning may actually be *whether we believe that learning is possible in the first place!*

Is intelligence and aptitude inborn or is it acquired?

Your answer to this single question, Dweck claims, is a better predictor of your success than any intelligence or aptitude you actually possess.

Why? Because from this single root belief branches many others.

If you have a fixed mindset, you believe that intelligence and ability are unchangeable. What does that imply?

- There's no real point in trying, because you'll only fail and embarrass yourself.
- Challenges are evidence that you're at a limit you can't go beyond. So you may as well give up and stick with what you know.
- If other people have been lucky and blessed with talent where you haven't, your only option is to be jealous of how unfair that is.
- You're born with it or you aren't, end of story. That means that if people offer feedback or criticism, they're actually attacking *you* as a person.
- Frustration, uncertainty, and difficulty—these are unpleasant and to be avoided. Why bother when your fate is predestined? If you're meant to do something, then it should be easy. If it's hard, that's proof it's not for you.

Your core belief about intelligence and ability shapes your beliefs about failure, hard work, and effort.

And *that* shapes how you respond to failure, how hard you work, and what efforts you make. Talk about a self-fulfilling prophecy!

Change the way you think about intelligence and ability, however, and everything else changes.

If you believe that growth is possible, then what does *that* imply?

- Failure, struggle, and hard work are just a normal part of life, can be and embraced as opportunities to learn and develop.
- Just because you don't succeed on your first try doesn't mean that you're doing anything wrong. You just haven't done it right *yet*.
- Feedback is super valuable and important. Mistakes help you fine-tune. You're eager to hear how you can become better, and you know that with effort you can be.
- Failure isn't personal. You can fail now, learn, then succeed later.
- Other people's success is interesting and admirable, and something to learn from. They remind you of what might be possible with effort.

The growth mindset is really a learning mindset.

The core attitude we take towards the process of learning itself is what will influence every part of that learning process.

With a fixed mindset, we play safe, avoid challenge, shirk hard work, and take failure personally. The fixed mindset actively limits our intellectual growth from the very start, shrinks our world, and undermines our resilience.

Want deep learning? Then begin by changing your attitude so that you see effort, persistence, and learning from failure as the true drivers of growth.

- You'll be more resilient in the face of setbacks.
- You'll stay committed to long-term goals.
- You'll be disciplined enough to engage fully with difficult material.
- You'll navigate challenges with patience, reflection, and stamina.

Whether we blame the school system, our upbringing, or our toxic cultural ideals, Dweck explains that unfortunately, most of us have a mindset that leans more towards the fixed.

The deep learning mindset is simply this: **Growth is always possible through effort.**

We *are* capable of change, adaptation, evolution, and transformation.

This is what learning is. And we are capable of it!

The *extent* to which we learn is determined more by our *attitude* than our *aptitude*.

Don't have a growth mindset? No problem! That's because *growth is always possible*, and if you don't *yet* have a skill, with effort, you can acquire it.

Let's look closer.

Reframe Failure as "Not Yet" Rather Than "I Can't"

Read back a few sentences and you'll see a magical three letter word that contains the very essence of the growth mindset: **yet**.

With this simple word, you express a lot:

- That you are in process. Growth takes time. You expect that.
- That incompleteness, awkwardness, failure, difficulty, or error in the present isn't permanent.
- That not knowing how to do something isn't a wrong turn on the path to knowing how to do it. It's a step *on* that path.

How do you interpret failure?

What is your response when you encounter something difficult, challenging, embarrassing, or confusing?

Fixed mindset: "This mistake is proof I'm not good enough."

Growth mindset: "Of course I'm not good enough yet, that's exactly why I'm learning! This mistake is teaching me."

Dweck explains it this way: "In one world, effort is a bad thing. It, like failure, means you're not smart or talented. If you were, you wouldn't need effort. In the other world, effort is what *makes* you smart or talented."

Dweck consistently explains that it's the growth mindset folks who actually end up on the far horizons of performance, knowledge, and success.

So, how do we reframe?

The next time you encounter a slip up or obstacle, just pause.

Now is your precious opportunity to start rewiring your thinking. How? Through the language you use:

- Instead of "I'm bad at math," say, "I don't understood this concept yet."
- Instead of "I can't do it," say, "I haven't figured out how to do it yet."
- Instead of "I was just born with two left feet," say, "I'm yet to master that move."

When we speak from a fixed mindset, it's like we slam a door shut in our mind. The end. Nothing more to see here.

Take a look:

"I'm not a good driver." → Grammatically closed. A judgment and foregone conclusion disguised as a factual statement. Game over.

"I'm learning to drive." → Present continuous tense suggests an *ongoing process.* Improvement is underway. Still open, still engaged. With effort, better driving awaits in your future. You just haven't arrived there yet. Doesn't that feel better?

More ways to reframe:

- Literally write the words "not yet" at the top of your notebook pages, or display them on a sticky note somewhere in your field of vision.
- Replace "failing" with "learning". You're not doing it wrong. You're figuring out how to do it right.
- Get into the habit of tracking *attempts*, not *achievements*. Keep a logbook of your activities without ranking them as outcomes:
    - What did you try?
    - What worked?
    - What didn't work?
    - What can you learn from what didn't work?
- Tell yourself: **Mistakes are just data**. Try stuff, gather that data, and learn.

Celebrate Effort, Not Just Outcomes

The fixed mindset is about performance. It's an ego thing. It's less about true learning and more about *appearing* intelligent, knowledgeable, and talented.

In the fixed mindset, we only take action when good outcomes are guaranteed. We go for easy wins and decline to make an attempt if there's a risk of looking like awkward beginners. Basically, the fixed mindset is all about the glamorous finish line... not the clumsy learning curve that leads there.

Maybe we imagine that natural-born geniuses get to enjoy effort-free success while the rest of us shy away, unwilling to do something if it means we'll be seen as not very good.

Maybe we believe that hard work doesn't count unless it amounts to a big prize at the end.

Let's turn this on its head!

A growth/deep learning mindset tells us that:

- Effort matters.
- Talent exists, but so what? We are not in control of that. What we are in control of is the amount of effort we make.
- We don't have to be good at something to make efforts. In fact, being bad at it is often the only way to get good at it.
- Just because some people can do something with little or no training, it

doesn't mean that we can't do the same *with* training. Sometimes, we can do it even better.

Tip: Avoid praising yourself for static traits, outcomes, and sheer luck. Instead, praise effort and hard work. That way, you always "win."

Instead of, "I'm good at programming," say, "I worked really hard on that project, and tried something new that worked well. I'm going to keep experimenting with it..."

Instead of, "I got 70% on the test," say, "I was a lot more intentional in my study process this time. Past papers are turning out to be really useful, but I'm still figuring out a good approach for the essay writing portion."

Consider keeping a **Process Journal.** At the end of every week, look at your efforts with neutral, curious eyes. **Reflect on your process, not your outcomes**:

- "What learning strategies have I used here?"
- "Have I tried anything new? How did that go?"
- "What am I learning about this process? And about myself?"
- "What has this taught me to try next time? What would I like to do more of?"
- "What did I work really hard on this week?"

- "Have I made any improvements to my overall strategy and method?"

For each journal entry, experiment with visual trackers to monitor and display your progress. For example, make a mark for every day you reflect on your process and follow through on your plans. You'll be motivated as you watch that winning streak grow longer.

Choose Challenges Over Comfort Zones

Within a fixed mindset, challenges are not opportunities to grow, but humiliating reminders of your deficiency. It's only logical that you would avoid trying something new and fall back instead on all those things that you're already good at, relying on a predictable sense of reward.

Comfortable and familiar? Yes.

Easy on the ego? Yes.

Likely to lead to learning growth and transformation? **Nope**.

Deep learning happens far outside your comfort zone. Deep learning is sometimes messy and hard. The irony is that fearing difficulty allows it to have power over us, whereas embracing it allows us to *use* it, so that we ultimately grow in confidence, courage, and capability. Then the thing actually becomes less difficult over time!

When you believe you can't really learn, that belief becomes reality. You choose things that are safe and easy. Then you stagnate.

Struggle...

Confusion...

Difficulty...

Uncertainty...

Awkwardness...

...what if you saw all this grappling and effort not as *threats*, but as *opportunities*?

To cultivate a growth mindset, we need to push back against the tendency to withdraw from challenge and instead approach it.

Once a week, deliberately give yourself a task that ever-so-slightly scares you:

- Tackle a task at *one level higher* than you'd ordinarily find comfortable.
- Begin every study session with the problems and exercises you find most challenging.
- Volunteer to give a talk, make a presentation, or do a task even though you're not perfectly confident with it yet.

Take a leap and figure it out along the way.
- If you're doing something and you find it easy, look for ways to make it more challenging. Find the growth.
- Stop avoiding those things you're bad at. Choose to do something precisely *because* you're bad at it!
- Feeling stuck? Try something new. Try that one thing you've told yourself you *can't* do. See what happens.
- Stop hiding your imperfect efforts and share your process with others. Ask for feedback. Let go of the myth of the lone artist, scientist, or athlete who must work in isolation until they're perfect.
- Take risks in the company of others. Let go of the "image". Stop seeking approval, forget about "genius", have a little grit, and simply refuse to take feedback personally.
- After a challenging task, don't worry about success or failure. Instead, ask yourself, **"What did I learn from that?"**

It's not about, "Can I do this?" or "Will I do it well enough?" or "How do I compare to other people?"

It's about, "What can I learn here?"

Choose what will help you grow, not what will help you feel safe in the moment. And remember, you don't have to do something perfectly or even well to learn from it.

Autotelic Activities: The Gateway to Deep Learning and Inner Growth

"An autotelic experience is very different from the feelings we typically have in the course of life. So much of what we ordinarily do has no value in itself, and we do it only because we have to do it, or because we expect some future benefit from it."

- Mihaly Csikszentmihalyi

To recap, a growth mindset = a deep learning mindset.

It's the belief that learning and growth is possible through effort, or even that "learning" is actually just the name we give to *effortful growth*. To learn is to grow, and to grow depends on belief in the possibility of change. So far so good.

Now here's another question: What's the payoff?

Growth towards what?

Learning about what?

Why?

To what end?

External rewards start early in life. Schoolchildren are given ready-made milestones to reach, and their progress through school is marked by grades, report cards, and gold stars.

When they grow up they work for the adult version of these rewards: paychecks, promotions, and prizes. For some, the reward is in the number of social media followers displayed after their name, for others it's a string of letters signaling academic accomplishments.

- Money
- Recognition
- Status
- Accolades
- Praise
- "Winning"
- Rewards
- Gold stars in report cards

These are all external motivators.

Psychologist Mihaly Csikszentmihalyi, the author of the 2008 bestseller *Flow: The Psychology of Optimal Experience*, explains how **high performers all share an interesting trait:** They are not driven by money or gold stars, but by something else entirely.

They are intrinsically motivated.

They are autotelic.

Auto = αὐτός, *autos*, "self"

Telos = τέλος, *telos*, "end"

The word *telos* comes to us from the Greek and has an Aristotelean history; it denotes something far bigger than a mere goal. Telos is about *purpose*. It's about the ultimate aim that something—or someone—is striving towards.

The autotelic person, then is someone whose purpose comes from within themselves, not from the outside.

According to Csikszentmihalyi, autotelic people are more likely to achieve "flow states", i.e., periods of total absorption where action and awareness merge, self-consciousness fades, and time seems to dissolve. **Flow states tend to arise from engaging in autotelic activities.**

Thus, there are two main sources of human motivation:

- **Extrinsic motivation**
    - Acting because you have been externally incentivized, encouraged, rewarded, or punished
    - The goal and payoff is the outcome, not the process
    - Trivial, short-lived

- Repetitive, mimetic, automatic action
- Shallow, transactional learning
- Feels like grind and force

- **Intrinsic motivation**
  - Acting from a genuine desire for meaning, value, purpose, passion, or curiosity
  - The goal is the process itself, not the outcome
  - Rich, sustainable
  - Intentional, original, and strategic action
  - Deep learning, learning for its own sake
  - Feels like it flows, not like it has to be forced

The message is clear: Deep learning is not about superficially boosting productivity or hustling harder than the next guy. It's about shifting our full attention into a totally new mode of engagement with the things that truly matter to us.

It's loving the process itself, not what we hope the process can give us.

The autotelic personality is the one most able to fuse with their goal-directed action and access deep learning, i.e., achieve a flow state. How does someone know they are in flow?

They are...

- Crystal clear on exactly what they are doing and the goal they're aiming for.
- Deeply engaged with the unfolding process itself; completely immersed.
- Finding joy in balancing their skill with the challenge at hand—and they don't mind sweating it.
- Single-minded. Completely, utterly undistracted. Not self-conscious in the least.
- Unconcerned with failure. They're not fearful nor are they arrogant. They're just not thinking about it.
- Enjoying themselves. They're not working—they're playing.
- Able to experience a kind of timelessness and ease.

As you can see, all of the above is about what's happening on the *inside*. The applause and accolades that come from the outside? When you're engrossed in autotelic activities, those things just don't matter.

Csikszentmihalyi describes it like this:

> "Such individuals lead vigorous lives, are open to a variety of experiences, keep on learning until the day they die, and have strong ties and commitments to other people and to the environment in which they live. They enjoy whatever they do,

even if tedious or difficult; they are hardly ever bored, and they can take in stride anything that comes their way. Perhaps their greatest strength is that they are in control of their lives."

Is it possible to become this kind of person?

Can we make our own learning process deeper and more autotelic? Absolutely!

Here's how.

Choose Goals That Are Intrinsically Meaningful

Think carefully about what is driving you.

Being extrinsically motivated means running along after a carrot. When the carrot moves, you move. But if the carrot disappears, so too does your effort and interest.

Let's be real: The world is currently maintained by people motivated by fear, social pressure, or the need to earn a paycheck.

Learning goals are no different. We may choose certain learning goals simply because they seem like things we should want. We may feel insecure and compelled to perform in some way: to earn approval, to demonstrate our value, to prove something, to elevate ourselves, or because we sincerely believe that achievement will fix whatever's wrong in our lives.

Autotelic people don't chase rewards that are dangled in front of them. Instead, they immerse themselves in what is meaningful and worthwhile, right now.

They are not on a treadmill, covering ground just to cover it. They are not mindlessly ticking boxes just to get to the bottom of a To Do list. Instead, they are driven by genuine enjoyment of each step.

Autotelic people can work hard even when

- The task is extremely difficult
- Gratification is delayed or entirely absent
- They receive little or no external reward from others

Switching to genuinely meaningful goals may feel weird at first if you've never really done it before.

The secret ingredient? Curiosity.

Find something you're truly curious about. What do you really, genuinely wish you understood better? Make *that* your quest, rather than just a grade, a reward, or a round of applause.

Tip: At the start of each week, ask yourself: "What do I truly want to learn this week?" Let that guide you. Align your external tasks with this internal desire. Then, notice what happens.

Design Your Work to Stretch Your Limits (But Not Break Them)

Csikszentmihalyi tells us that "the best moments usually occur when a person's body or mind is stretched to its limits in a voluntary effort to something difficult and worthwhile."

Note: stretched to the limits—not beyond them.

Too little challenge = stagnation, boredom, superficiality, loss of passion.

Too much challenge = overwhelm, stress, resentment, loss of confidence.

The sweet spot in the middle is where we are neither bored nor anxious, but fully *enjoying* our work.

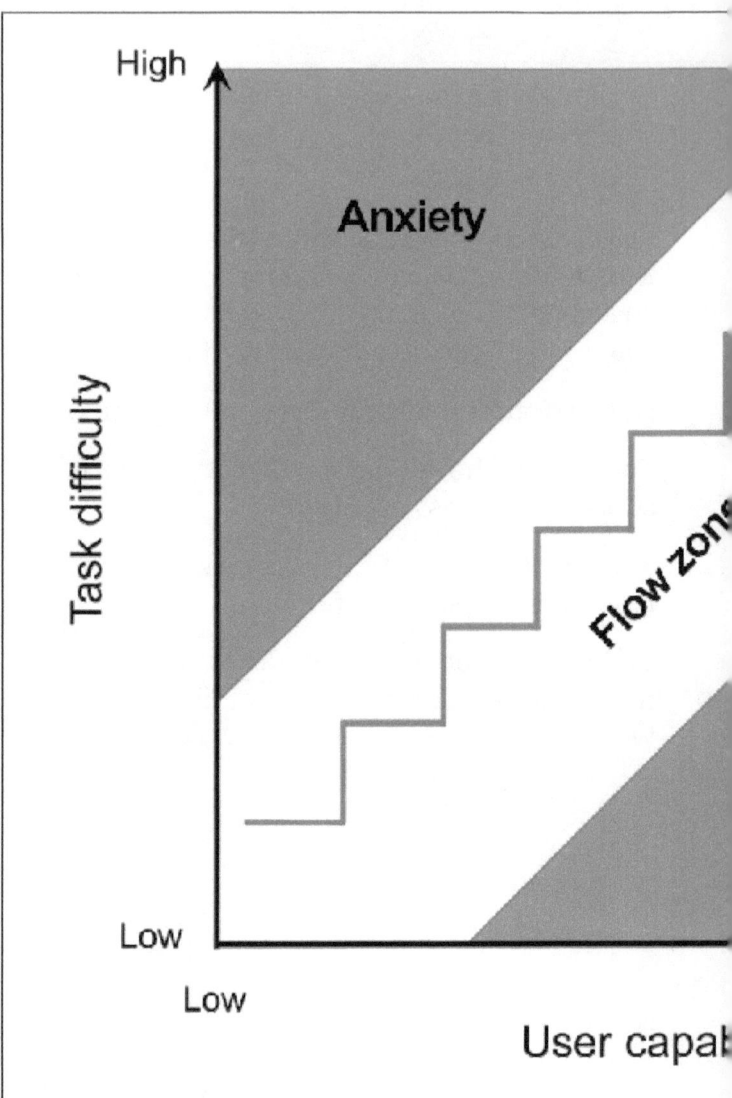

Figure adapted from Csikszentmihalyi, 1990, Harper & Row.

Flow states, deep work, and deep learning occur in a middle zone where the difficulty of a task and your own skill level are in optimal ranges.

A few points:

- Every task you do falls somewhere in this chart.
- Your skill level is unique and varies day by day.
- The difficulty level is subjective—two people will have two different perceptions of a task's difficulty

It is not about your objective skill level or the difficulty of the task. It is about their *relationship* and relative proportion to one another. That means that you can technically find a flow state in *any* task, no matter who you are.

Your goal: Match the challenge of what you're doing to your current skill level.

Periodically check in to see how you're feeling (yes, feedback about your cognitive performance will come via emotional channels).

- **Feel *bored*?** That's a sign to *increase the challenge* until you're in the flow zone again.
- **Feel *anxious*?** That's a sign to *decrease the challenge* until you're in the flow zone again.

What about making changes to skill level? If we're bored, we can theoretically reduce our skill level, but that's not usually an option for obvious reasons.

If we're anxious we can relieve that stress by increasing our skill level, but this may not always be possible, at least not immediately. Increasing skill is naturally the goal, but it usually only happens when in the flow zone anyway.

Our main focus should be on modifying the degree of challenge. By fine-tuning task difficulty, we can keep ourselves in that narrow flow state corridor.

Invest Your Full Attention and Eliminate Distractions

Autotelic, deep work, and deep learning require undivided attention.

Being in a flow state means we are totally absorbed in a task, have fully invested our attention and energy, and are oblivious to distractions. If an interruption is irrelevant to our task, it just bounces off our awareness.

To get into this state in the first place, however, we need to be intentional about protecting our attention and avoiding distraction.

- Allocate non-negotiable time blocks for a task (say, 60 or 90 minutes) and set an alarm.
- Mentally make the commitment to yourself: "I am doing this task now, and this task *only*."
- Put all notifications and devices on silent, shut the door, and let everyone know not to disturb you. No phones, no scrolling breaks, no multitasking.
- If your mind wanders off task, pull your attention right back again.

Enjoy the Process and Track Feedback, Not Just Results

If it's not enjoyable, it's not autotelic, and it's not flow.

"Enjoyable" doesn't mean it's entertaining or feels like a holiday. Flow enjoyment is a rich sense of *fulfilment* that stems from:

- Having clear goals
- Receiving immediate feedback whenever you move closer to that goal
- A balance between difficulty and skill

Take note: Overly easy tasks are *not* enjoyable or satisfying! Neither are overly difficult tasks. You don't want low-value, low-hanging fruit, nor do you want to demoralize yourself with something above your ability. Enjoyment is the game you play in the middle.

If it doesn't feel like a game? Make a few tweaks:

- **Clear goals**: Do you know what you're doing and why? Are these meaningful goals and are they super, ultra, crystal clear in your mind? Is it obvious to you how your current efforts lead directly to the goal?
- **Immediate feedback**: Make sure that you're acknowledging and rewarding each milestone and achievement as soon as possible after you've reached it. For example, don't complete a mock exam and grade it all at the end, but check your answer after each question. Those little dopamine hits make you feel like you're hot on the trail of the learning process.
- **Balance**: Keep checking in with yourself. What work conditions feel challenging but fun? When did you feel bored and why? What challenge inspired you and what felt overwhelming? Adjust accordingly.

Deep, autotelic work requires intrinsic motivation, meaningful goals, an equilibrium between skill and difficulty, and a sincere sense of enjoyment, fun, or play.

Metacognition: The Key to Smarter, Deeper Learning

"Metacognition asks the question: What do I know about how I learn and think that will help me with this new situation?"

- **Howard Pitler**

Learning is not about what you know or don't know.

It's not about inborn skill, luck, or talent.

It's about *how you think.*

The ability to think about how you think is called metacognition, and it's a kind of uber-skill that helps us learn how to learn.

Metacognition is being aware of your own thought processes, and therefore being able to manage, direct, and improve them. You have a kind of second brain which can become conscious of and think about the first.

People who are masters of deep learning are first masters of metacognition:

- They can process information and understand how they themselves are doing that processing.
- They can reflect on their processes.

- They can make the conscious choices to observe, experiment, implement, and change strategies.

Metacognition is the higher organizing principle behind every peak performance or high achievement.

Repetition, rote memorization, mimicry, and habit are simply not good enough. These things are always limited to a narrow range of activities.

Metacognition, however, is the only and ultimate transferable skill—it is the one tool we can use in every endeavor we attempt.

This is why we began our book not with a consideration of different techniques and methods, but with an exploration of the underlying mindset that generates and empowers a person to use them skillfully and intelligently.

Growth mindset? Check.

Autotelic orientation? Check.

Now let's explore ways to cultivate the power of metacognition.

Practice Self-Monitoring Before, During, and After Tasks

Metacognition isn't something you slip into now and again. Ideally it should be a constant state of mind that you bring to your work from start to finish. Actually, it should kick in even *before* you begin and continue even *after* you've finished!

Metacognition is about being aware of what you are doing in the moment. This self-awareness takes the form of continuous self-monitoring.

No, you're not just mentally spying on yourself all day long for fun or chipping in with negative self-talk. You're doing it so you can:

- Notice what is happening
- Evaluate what is happening
- Develop and utilize plans, strategies, and techniques
- Make adjustments
- Monitor your progress as you go

Importantly, you are not monitoring your first-order performance on the task. You are monitoring the learning process itself.

See if you can spot the difference:

"I got 80% on the quiz."

"I'm up from 70% last week, which suggests that the flashcards I've been experimenting with may be working better for me than rote memorizing from the book."

You can strengthen the self-monitoring habit using a written Progress Journal, and later internalize it as a purely mental habit. It does not take long to pause and quickly run through the following questions:

- **Self-monitor BEFORE a task (1-2 minutes before beginning)**
    o "What am I trying to achieve during this session?"
    o "What is my strategy or plan of approach? Why? Is that the best way forward?"
    o "What do I already know about this topic that I can build on?"
    o "What obstacles or difficulties do I anticipate? How can I pre-empt them?"
- **Self-monitor DURING a task (every 10 minutes or so while you work)**
    o "Do I *actually* understand this, or am I just going through the motions?"
    o "Is what I'm doing actually working? Why or why not?"
    o "What do I have available to me right now to do better?"
    o "Can I make small adjustments or tweaks right now?"
- **Self-monitoring AFTER a task (1-2 minutes after you finish)**
    o "What worked well during that session? Why?"

- "How can I plan to do more of it next time?"
- "Where am I still stuck? How can I find out more? What do I want to try next time?"
- "Did I achieve what I set out to achieve? Why or why not? What does that tell me?"

Later in our book, we'll explore several practical ways to plan, memorize, understand, and retain material, but for now we are focusing simply on the habit of awareness and metacognition.

Use Strategy-Based Thinking to Solve Problems

In battle, opposing sides each possess military strength, intelligence, and power. But the decisive factor is usually the strategy employed—i.e. the detailed plan for *how to use* all that strength, intelligence, and power.

Working harder only gets you so far.

Working smarter requires strategy—a detailed plan of action.

Importantly, a tool on its own does not constitute strategy; what matters is our deliberate *use* of that tool.

Mind maps, flashcards, and apps are just tools. Our conscious decisions about how we'll use them to our own purpose is *strategy*.

When you are faced with a problem (and really, converting ignorance to understanding is the problem of problems) just pause for a moment.

- Don't rush in to start using this or that tool
- Don't default to pre-existing systems and gimmicks
- Don't automatically fall back on old habits just because that's what you did last time

Instead, try "talking yourself through" a problem. Have strategy-based thinking, rather than relying on rote or brute force. Be the commander-in-chief and purposefully rally your mental resources, make a plan, and follow it through.

For example, imagine you're tackling a math problem. Instead of barging ahead with whatever knee-jerk response comes to mind, talk yourself through:

> *"OK, let's start at the beginning. What is this question actually asking me to do? What kind of math problem is this? Let me make a few notes here in the margin about everything I know, and everything I'm asked to figure out. OK, that's done. This*

still seems hard. What am I missing? Ah, maybe I need to separately determine the missing information. Do I need a formula? No, I don't think that will work here. OK, I see my first step. Let me do this, then that, then the last thing. OK, that's done. Let me double check. Do my units match up? Let me read the question again and see if my answer makes sense..."

Here, metacognition and strategy-based thinking are not separate activities you do alongside the work—it's an *ongoing* way of doing the work.

Slow down.

Be deliberate.

See thoughts and actions as choices.

Always seek to understand the *why* and not just the *how*.

Discover What Works Best for You as a Learner

When we learn, we gain fresh insight and understanding about something we were previously ignorant about.

When we learn about how we learn, we gain fresh insight into *ourselves*.

We all learn differently. Your brain, your personality, your schedule, your lifestyle, your strengths, your limitations, your goals, your values... all of these are unique to you, and they may change over the course of your life.

With metacognition, you **discover what works for you.**

Too many of us observe others having success with this or that tool, and assume that if we also use that tool, we'll get the same success. But the tool likely worked for that person... *because it worked for that person.* You'll have success too, when you find what works best for you.

When you constantly monitor yourself and ask questions about your process, you will begin to notice patterns. For example:

- You notice you perform better at 11am than at 3pm.
- You notice that you work more quickly with method 1 than method 2, but make more mistakes.
- You notice that your stress levels are sky-high when there's a time limit.
- You notice that you're distracted less when watching videos than when reading.
- You notice that you prefer this speaker over that one.

- You notice that you have greater stamina when you take mini breaks all throughout the work session.

...and so on.

Once you've noticed a pattern, then what?

Then it's time to use strategy-based thinking. **Move towards what works, and away from what doesn't.** Ask questions. Conduct mini-experiments, gather data, and adjust your process as you go.

For example, you notice that you seem to grasp new concepts quickest when you read a quick summary first, then listen to an explainer video with plenty of real examples. You ask, "Is it the case that a blend of audio and visual data works best?"

You test this out by playing around with keeping the video tutorial subtitles on vs. off. You do a trial where you pause every five minutes of the video to jot down notes and summary points. Then you notice more patterns, and ask more questions, making more adjustments as you go…

You keep a record of everything you're learning, perhaps compiling a list called "What works for me."

If it stops working, no big deal. You can change your approach as you change, and as your skill level, confidence, and goals change.

This way, you are not just learning, but also learning how to learn.

You're no longer

- A passive consumer of information
- A student blindly following a curriculum you don't understand
- A person driven solely by external pressures

Instead you become

- An independent thinker
- A resilient problem-solver
- A self-directed learner

Deliberate Practice for Deep Learning: Quality Over Quantity

"The reason that most people don't possess these extraordinary physical capabilities isn't because they don't have the capacity for them, but rather because they're satisfied to live in the comfortable rut of homeostasis and never do the work that is required to get out of it. They live in the world of "good enough." The same thing is true for all the mental activities we engage in."

- **Anders Ericsson and Robert Pool, *Peak: Secrets from the New Science of Expertise***

Let's begin this chapter with an unflattering truth: Sometimes, we perform at a level much lower than what we're capable of, because it'll do. We're distracted and trapped in superficial activities, forfeiting *Excellent* because we're content with *Satisfactory*.

This even applies to the concept of practice, which is precisely the arena in which we should be stretching, pushing, expanding, and reaching.

We say that we're engaged in practice, but what we're really doing is going through the motions.

Practice doesn't really make perfect. Deliberate, intentional, and strategic practice makes perfect.

On the other hand, routine, shallow, and mindless practice makes... well, not much.

Practice is a necessary condition for excellence, but not all practice is created equal.

Anders Ericsson was the originator of the "10,000 hours rule", i.e., the idea that true mastery is acquired after around 10,000 hours of deliberate practice. While Malcolm Gladwell popularized the idea, it was Ericsson, a Swedish psychologist and performance expert, that laid the real groundwork and did the research.

Whether it was expertise in sports, music, medicine, or chess, Ericsson had a question: What makes an expert performer?

- Personality?
- Intelligence?
- Training?
- Raw talent?
- Genetics?

Ericsson found that expert performers had something in common: *they all engaged in extended periods of high concentration practice, beyond their comfort zone.*

While everyone focused on the 10,000 hours, they missed the important part of Ericsson's message—it's not the number of hours, but what you do with them.

When it comes to practice, it's **quality over quantity** every time. As they say, it's not what you do, it's the way that you do it.

Gladwell might have misrepresented Ericsson's findings. The goal is never to mindlessly rack up 10,000 hours. That's because it's not the amount of practice time that makes you progress, but the amount of practice time *you spend out of your comfort zone.*

It may *feel* good to repeat the same action over and over, especially if that action is "good enough" and fairly easy for you, but this is not deep learning.

It's not the path to excellence.

We certainly need all the other important ingredients (commitment, focused attention, enjoyment, meaningful goals, internal motivation, a mentor, and so on) but day to day, it all comes together in the *how* of deliberate practice.

We learn when we push ourselves. We learn when we identify problems and knowledge gaps, and use strategic thinking to plug them up, using feedback and our own internal motivation to drive us. Deliberate practice is the surest path to deep learning, real progress, lasting retention, and cognitive transformation.

Ericsson's actual findings show that we **get better when we sustain consistent, high-quality practice just outside our comfort zone.**

(By the way, the comfort zone is not just a figure of speech, but a real state of mind. We'll be exploring exactly what this state of mind is in Chapter 2).

In *The Little Book of Talent*, Daniel Coyle puts it this way:

> "There is a place, right on the edge of your ability, where you learn best and fastest. It's called the sweet spot... The underlying pattern is the same: Seek out ways to stretch yourself. Play on the edges of your competence."

Let's take a look at three practical ways to find that sweet spot, and make deliberate practice a way of life. Remember—**we don't count hours; we make the hours count.**

Focus on Specific, Measurable Micro-Goals

Our deliberate intention needs to be like a scalpel—specific, targeted, sharp.

We need to know *exactly* what we're doing, how well we're doing it, how to improve it, and how to measure that progress.

When we are **precise** in this way, we make real use of the time we have, and cut out everything that is automatic, mindless, or wasteful.

Imagine that you're learning to play the piano.

Without specific and measurable goals, it may look like this:

- You sit down and, having not made any plan, end up playing the first thing that comes to your mind—your favorite and well-practiced piece. You repeat this a few times.

- You think "maybe I should do scales or something" so you try a few, get bored, then wander onto something else.
- You take a look at a new piece you'd like to learn, and bumble aimlessly through the first few bars. It's hard!
- You practice the well-loved piece a few more times for fun, think "I'm really nailing this" and just like that an hour has passed.

Though you're busily doing something every minute of this hour, after six months of practice you seem not to have made the slightest bit of improvement. Worse still, you think, "I've plateaued. This must just be as good as I can get. Maybe I'm not a very good pianist."

Compare:

- You sit down and play your favorite piece, but just to warm up your fingers. This encourages you and reminds you of how far you've come.
- Next, scales. You know exactly which ones, because you're on a 12-week plan.
- Within 15 minutes you're ready to tackle the new piece. You practice slowly and deliberately for the next 15 minutes, carefully isolating tiny portions and drilling them until they're smooth, before moving onto the next tiny portion.

- You put all the pieces together and drill the entire thing, first slowly then at natural speed. You make notes about what worked technique-wise, and scribble down your plan for your next session.
- At the end of the hour, you're exhausted, but satisfied. Your progress is visible. Your improvement can be tracked. There's no guesswork here—you're training with intention.

At the end of six months, you've acquired the next piece and can play it comfortably. But you're not surprised by this—it's exactly what you *planned* to do!

Practice at the Edge of Your Comfort Zone

Do you ever feel bored during practice?

Do you ever notice yourself kind of zoning out or slipping into autopilot?

That's a sign! You're in your comfort zone, not your deep learning zone. The clock may be ticking... but you are *not* improving.

Recall the diagram showing the narrow corridor of Flow state nestled between too challenging and not challenging enough. We need to practice in that lively middle zone—stretching our capacity far enough that we're learning, but not so far that we're overwhelmed.

Warning: Mindless practice may *feel* good. But be careful. Just because it's fun to keep repeating all those things you're already good at, it doesn't mean you're actually being productive. You're not gaining.

- Don't endlessly return to all those topics you're already comfortable and familiar with.
- Avoid prioritizing those tasks that you're naturally good at.
- Let go of ideas about what your current best can be—don't camp out forever at your personal best.

Instead, Ericsson encourages people to stay on the edge of what they can do. Practice should be about *constant tension* in that optimal zone.

- Find your weakest areas and focus on improving those.
- Get feedback on what you can improve.
- See your current skill level as just that—current, but actively being extended with every practice.

Seek that space where you are **struggling productively**. An hour spent in this zone will yield ten times as much deep learning as an hour spent reinforcing all those same old mental pathways you've already embedded into your brain.

Drilling existing knowledge *is* valuable—but revising is not learning.

Structure Practice With Purpose, Feedback, and Recovery

Deliberate practice is iterative, not repetitive.

The conventional misunderstanding around the 10,000 hours concept makes it seem that if you merely do the same thing over and over again for long enough, you'll eventually become an expert at it.

Not true!

There is no virtue in endlessly grinding through hours and hours of repetition. You are not learning. You are not improving. You are just going through the motions.

What *does* help?

Deliberate practice is *mindful*, not *mindless*

This means it's cognitively demanding, which means you can't realistically sustain sessions longer than 60—90 minutes. To recap, deliberate practice is:

- Short, focused, and high quality
- Guided by immediate feedback
- Followed by effective recovery

As an example, consider how you might learn a language.

Shallow, ineffectual "grinding" practice = working for hours on long, tedious, rote memorization of strings of new vocabulary words, most of which you already know.

Deep, effective deliberate practice looks different:

- **Short, focused, and high quality**. You create a detailed, deliberate plan for an hour study session, and time block it in advance in your calendar. You choose a time when you're most alert, you cut out distractions, and you run through an initial grounding and focusing routine.
- **Immediate feedback.** You strategically choose a particular technique (flashcards) to drill vocabulary words and precisely identify the ones you find most difficult. The flashcards you already know are removed from the deck, so that you are only practicing with those you have yet to master. You stay at the edge of your comfort zone by continually working on those words you struggle with, not those you already find easy.

- **Effective recovery.** You end the hour session with a few minutes of review, determining what worked, what didn't, and what you want to do next time. You make a few notes, see whether your goals have been met, then rest well to give your brain time to consolidate and lock in those gains.

If you repeat the above process—which is **iterative, intelligent, and adaptive**—then you literally cannot help but learn!

If you merely repeat the same string of actions over and over, then all you are doing is entrenching mediocrity. This is anti-learning.

Many people hear about the 10,000-hour rule and quietly conclude, "*That's* how long it takes to get good at something? Clearly there's no point in starting. I don't have the time."

The great thing about deliberate practice is that it *doesn't* eat up unimaginable amounts of time, because it's quality over quantity. **Deep learning is alive, active, and responsive**. **Never mechanical**. It's an alert, engaged state of being that keeps our efforts closely tracking the "growing tip" of our attentive awareness.

- Note your current skill level. Constantly be finding ways to jump up to the next level.

- Note what you're doing wrong. Constantly look for ways to measure that performance and improve on it.
- Note what you are currently achieving. Constantly look for ways to leverage that.
- Note the components and elements of what you're trying to learn and methodically move through each one. Be structured. Be targeted.
- Note how your performance compares against your goals. Constantly find ways to challenge yourself, being 10% or even 1% better than you were last time.

You are not performing, but learning, which means that you will be constantly exposed to mistakes, errors, and awkwardness.

Celebrate that! It's evidence that you're in the learning zone.

Remember, "**The master has failed more times than the beginner has even tried**." Learning may be unpleasant, frustrating, and hard going sometimes.

But that's the point.

If you're too comfortable, you're simply not growing.

Summary

- Deep learning is not about what you *do*, but how you *think*. **Knowing how to learn is the ultimate transferable skill.**
- The **growth mindset** sees intelligence and ability as acquirable, and growth is possible. Thus, effort is expected, and failure embraced as a normal part of learning.
- Focus on **process, not outcomes**, and celebrate **hard work, not perfection**. Use the magic growth mindset word "**yet**." Remember that comfort zones may feel good, but they don't spur learning.
- **Be autotelic**. It's about meaning, purpose, and values that you proactively choose for yourself. Intrinsic motivation + curiosity + sufficient challenge = flow state.
- **The keep to deep learning is metacognition**—thinking about thinking and learning about learning. Self-monitor, be strategic, and create a learning protocol that fits you and your unique goals, temperament, and limitations.
- Practice doesn't really make perfect. **Deliberate, intentional, and strategic practice** makes perfect. Set micro goals and track yourself.
- We get better when we sustain **consistent, high-quality practice just outside our comfort zone**.

- **Deliberate practice is iterative, not repetitive. It is alive, active, and responsive**. Seek immediate feedback and constant adjustment, paired with effective recovery.

Chapter 2: What True Learning Looks Like

Unlocking Deep Learning Through Vygotsky's Zone of Proximal Development

"One must develop an instinct for what one can just barely achieve through one's greatest efforts."

- **Albert Einstein**

While you've heard of the term *comfort zone*, have you ever heard of the "zone of proximal development"?

Russian psychologist Lev Vygotsky created one of the most influential frameworks for understanding what learning actually is and how it unfolds. Deep learning isn't just accumulating facts and details; rather, it's a complex and iterative process of acquiring real understanding. **Learning is a developmental process.**

Very briefly, the Zone of Proximal Development (ZPD) is a kind of sweet spot; it's the range of abilities that a person can achieve with help. There are three main "zones":

1. Those things you can easily do on your own.
2. Those things you cannot do at all (even with help).
3. Those things you can't do alone, but can *if* you have support, guidance, and teachings from an expert.

The ZPD is all about this third zone.

Think about it: How does one learn to do what they cannot do? How does one understand what one cannot understand? How does one know what they don't know?

For Vygotsky, you need a bridge. You need "mental training wheels."

Now, conventional understanding sees learning as a kind of private, independent act. We see children sitting at individual school desks, working in isolation, relying only on their own intellectual resources.

But what if this isn't how learning occurs at all?

Vygotsky's genius was to understand that real development actually unfolds in context and is always scaffolded on existing social knowledge. To put this differently, *our learning is most effective and transformative when others are helping us.*

Vygotsky claimed that learning is a sociocultural phenomenon, and that a "more knowledgeable other" could keep people in that critical deep learning zone.

This more knowledgeable other could be:

- A teacher
- A mentor
- A peer

Do they know just a teeny bit more than you currently do? Then they can act as a more knowledgeable other. The idea is that **you mimic, follow, and eventually internalize their mastery as your own.**

Vygotsky's theory can get complex, but applying his insights to our own learning process is fairly straightforward. Let's take a look.

Learn Just Beyond Your Comfort Zone—with Guidance

Where does learning occur?

Not in that zone where you can already do a task, nor in that zone where you can't do it, even with help.

No, learning occurs in that special sweet spot between competence and ignorance, that gray zone between "I can" and "I can't."

If a task is too easy = No learning.

If a task is too hard = No learning.

Dwelling on the stuff you can already do feels good, and forcing yourself to take on tasks that are beyond you feels bad. But being right in the middle? That feels **challenging but doable**.

You find it hard, but not impossible.

You don't fully understand the concept, but you *almost* get it.

You can't coordinate your muscles to perform the movement just yet, but you can see how someone else does it, and you're *almost* able to copy them.

This is where the magic happens!

- **Step 1:** A more knowledgeable "other" acts like your training wheels. They may say, "Watch how I do it."
- **Step 2:** You watch. Then you try, but with their help. They "hold your hand" through it.
- **Step 3:** After some time, you try it by yourself, without the training wheels.
- **Step 4:** You adjust, correct, improve. Gradually, it's as though your mentor's voice is becoming your own, and you're able to talk to yourself as though they were talking to you.
- **Step 5:** Soon, that voice disappears all together—because you're doing the

thing. The skill or knowledge is now your own.

Ideally, teachers, tutors, mentors, and trainers would understand ZPD theory and know how to work alongside their students so that they were always squarely inside the deep learning zone.

What about those of us who are trying to teach ourselves, or those who haven't been blessed with good teachers or mentors?

No problem. Simply understanding Vygotsky's theory can help you learn better, no matter what your constraints are:

- First things first: **Pay very close attention to which zone you're in**. Note your emotions and stress levels. *Easy* is fun but you don't want easy. You don't want *impossible,* either. Aim for "productively challenged." This is the flow state.
- Too easy? Up the challenge. Too hard? Lower the challenge, and/or seek a knowledgeable other to walk you through, step by step.
- Learning platforms like Exercism, Codecademy, or Khan Academy can supply both guidance, support, challenges, and hints for when you're stuck.
- **Actively seek help and support**. Ask people to walk you through their process.

Sometimes, someone who has only recently learned what you have yet to learn is a better teacher than a long-standing expert—because that learning is still fresh in their minds.

- Aim for "just in time" learning rather than "just in case" learning. Learn what you need to at a given level and then move on ASAP. Don't hang around collecting gold stars—level up as soon as humanly possible.

The aim is to feel stretched, not stuck.

How do you know you're in the zone?

- You're making mistakes—but not the same ones over and over.
- You're improving, even if slowly.
- Your questions and challenges are changing over time.
- You feel engaged and spurred on.
- You're feeling that *almost* vibe—like you're just on the cusp of getting it!

Use Scaffolding Strategies That Match Your Learning Stage

When constructing a physical building, you need a temporary/transitional building for support—scaffolding. In the same way, cognitive buildings require support while you work to build a new skill or acquire new knowledge.

As you build competency, you take down the old scaffolding and built it again at the next level up.

Good scaffolding is:

- Temporary
- Personalized

Scaffolding for cognitive buildings includes things like

- Tools
- Resources
- Exercises
- Instructions
- Any tips, tricks, or hacks that act as guard rails and training wheels

In a traditional learning context, it's the more knowledgeable other that uses scaffolding to assist their student. You can supply your own scaffolds, however:

Guided examples. Work through a few math problems with the full solution alongside, then attempt similar problems on your own, following that method.

Use progressive modeling. Ask a mentor to show you the first step of a sports maneuver, do the second part together as a team, and follow through to complete the final part yourself.

Milestones and feedback. Break a musical piece down into many smaller chunks. Practice each chunk, get feedback, then move onto the next.

Learn to instruct yourself. Ask for guided instructions on a dance move, then do the move as you hear the instructions, then attempt the move while mentally telling yourself the instructions as you go. Alternatively, make yourself walk through your own thought process, "What am I doing now? What comes next? OK, now take this over here and…"

Use templates. If you're learning to write amazing essays, create a standard template that you use for the first few times, before you've internalized that structure.

Stay aware. Deep learning in the ZPD requires metacognition. Pause frequently for self-assessment. How are you doing?

Use tools. Make liberal use of visualizations, charts, videos, checklists, metaphors, analogies, visual aids, stories, and diagrams to help you initially grasp new concepts.

Leverage Peer Learning and Dialogue to Internalize Understanding

One of Vygotsky's most important perceptions is that learning is *social before it becomes internal*. Before we "own" a skill in our own minds, we often process it first through conversations with others.

External dialogue becomes internal thought process.

- Learning a language? Don't sit in isolation running through flashcards—join a real-life language exchange group and engage with native speakers and fellow learners.
- Learning a new academic subject? Study alongside peers and *work with them* through challenging abstract concepts.
- Learning to use a new piece of software or tool at work? Ask a colleague to sit down with you and create a short project together.

The idea is not that other people are doing the task for you; rather, you are making the learning process richer and more memorable. By talking out loud through problems with others, we improve our ability to process those same ideas *internally*. We create new neural pathways.

We will explore the "teach yourself" idea more fully in a later chapter, but for now, here's a fun way to leverage peer-learning:

- **Step 1:** Try explaining a new concept while your study partner listens.
- **Step 2:** They ask you clarifying questions, seek elaboration, or challenge your blind spots.

- **Step 3:** You work together to refine your explanation, noting what you still need to do to improve your understanding.
- **Step 4:** You switch places and continue with the same or a different topic.

You may be surprised that whenever you think of this topic, even years later, you can still hear the voice of your study partner in your head!

Instructional Scaffolding: Building Pathways to Deep Learning

Learning is not always linear—sometimes it builds on itself, layer by layer, each new achievement supported by the previous one. This is called **scaffolding**, and the more intentional you are when making your own scaffolds, the more resilient the knowledge structures will be that you create.

Use the "I Do—We Do—You Do" Framework to Move from Dependence to Independence

Big tasks can be intimidating. It's like staring at a tall tower and wondering how you'll ever get to the top.

Good scaffolding is seeing that someone has already gone before you, and built a staircase to spiral around the outside of that tower. Yes, you still have to climb to get to the top, but there's a *route*, and you can see exactly what to do, one step at a time.

The "I Do—We Do—You Do" Framework is a helpful way of structuring your process:

I DO—the "I" here can be understood as the teacher or the more knowledgeable other. Watch someone else go up the staircase and see how they do it. Watch a video where someone models a technique or walks you through a process. Pay close attention to what the experts do.

Say out loud to yourself: "They're doing X. Look at how they Y. Watch what they do with Z..."

WE DO—practice the task alongside a more knowledgeable other. Hold their hand as you walk with them up the tower. Now, you are not just watching them but matching your movements to theirs. Do the task but use supports like templates, guides, partially completed examples, or other safety nets and training wheels.

Say out loud to yourself: "Let's do X together. Then it's Y. This is how we move onto Z..."

YOU DO—now it's your turn to climb the tower yourself, independently. Remember everything you've seen and learned. You are no longer watching the knowledgeable other, you are embodying them.

Say out loud to yourself: "OK, try to remember how it goes. First it's X, then I go to Y... now I carefully do Z just as I saw it..."

The idea is that you never need to dive into independent activity from the get-go. Instead, learning is graded and gradual:

Observe others doing it → do it yourself, but with help → do it independently.

By verbalizing the process through step-by-step instructions, you gradually **internalize the process** and make it your own, bringing those instructions from *out there* to *in here*.

Eventually, you don't need to speak the process out loud anymore because you have fully taken it in—it's yours.

- **Keep breaking tasks down into chunks.** Not only will this be psychologically more manageable, but it also provides a sense of process—that staircase may be long, but it's just one simple step after another.
- **Take as long as you need to practice with support.** Wean yourself off gradually. Is a step too big? Break it down further. Does a task still feel too difficult? Practice a little longer with training wheels.
- **Use social interaction to bootstrap your learning process.** Talk through

your thinking, whether that's with a peer or a mentor. Verbal communication makes you slow down and deliberate—even if you're alone and have to imagine an audience or study partner!

Spaced Repetition: A Simple Path to Deep Learning

"Repetition is the mother of all learning."

- **Latin proverb**

Comprehension is one thing. But if you don't **retain** what you learn, you cannot be said to have learned anything.

Deep learning has to be learning that sticks, and getting new information to stick requires much more than just exposure to that information.

Have you ever had a really good study session, then discovered a few days later that almost everything you thought you had "learned" had completely flown out of your head?

German psychologist Hermann Ebbinghaus has a theory about why this happens. In the 1880s his research found that test participants' recall for a string of nonsense syllables steadily degraded over time:

- **After 1 hour, 50% of what we've learned is forgotten**
- **After 24 hours, 70% of what we've learned is forgotten**
- **After 1 week, 90% of what we've learned is forgotten**

Plotted on a graph, this has come to be called the "Forgetting Curve" and it's as discouraging as it looks.

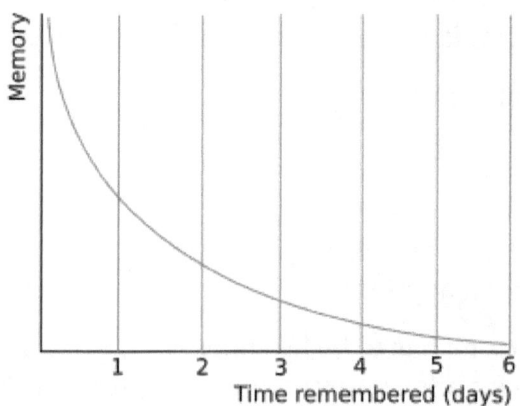

What can be done?

Here's a more encouraging graph:

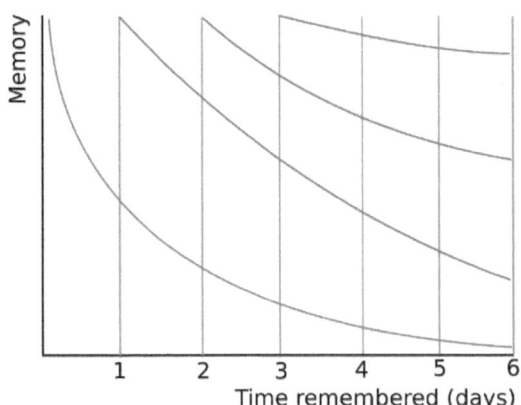

The Forgetting Curve

Whenever you review information, you temporarily boost your recall back to 100% again. What's more, with every review, the Forgetting Curve grows less steep, meaning you forget at a slower and slower rate. In other words, you're committing that information more securely into your long-term memory.

This method of temporarily boosting memory with fresh retrievals is called spaced repetition, or alternatively **distributed practice**, and it's the surest way to combat the natural tendency to forget newly acquired information.

Memory decay is a fact of life, but with a little strategy, we can offset it and achieve lasting knowledge retention.

When it comes to memory, it's never "one and done." Your brain needs **time** to absorb and reinforce new information. It also needs **repetition**.

Spaced repetition means giving our brains enough opportunity to process and formalize new neural connections. Comprehension and understanding are important, but it's purposeful repetition that allows us to *bank* that new understanding.

Review Key Information at Strategic Intervals

Your brain's default state is to forget—and that's a *good* thing. Think of it this way: Your brain wants to reserve as much of its power as possible for those tasks and demands that are most current. It's about priorities. If something's not current, your brain has no reason to hold onto it!

The easy loophole? Make things current!

Strategically review things before you have the chance to forget them. Keep reviewing until things become more permanent long-term memories.

Strategic review does not have to be complicated to be effective.

First question: "How long should my intervals be?"

The answer to that depends on:

- Your goals and deadlines. Urgent tasks = shorter intervals
- Difficulty and complexity. More complex = shorter intervals
- Preference and personality. Some of us just like longer intervals, some shorter.

Your intervals can generally follow the same shape as the Forgetting Curve, gradually tapering off over time. Because you risk losing most of what you've just learned in the day or so after learning it, this is where you should intensify your repetition practice:

- Day 0: First exposure
- Day 1: First repetition
- Day 2: Second repetition
- Day 4: Third repetition
- Day 8: Fourth repetition
- Day 16: Fifth repetition
- Day 32: Sixth repetition
- Etc.

Some claim that each interval should be roughly twice as long as the previous one, others that after seven repetitions you will have flattened the Forgetting Curve enough and can move on. The truth is that **your individual results will vary,** so continually evaluate your progress and adjust according to *your* retention rate.

Second question: "What do I have to review?"

The answer to this is: Only *key* information. Recall broad outlines, major themes, and central ideas. Not everything plus the kitchen sink.

Use Active Recall Instead of Passive Review

Warning: Lots of activities that call themselves "recall" actually have nothing to do with strengthening your memory:

- Highlighting
- Re-reading
- "Going over" notes

These things tend not to be **active recall.** They don't engage your memory and so they don't cultivate it.

Active recall = a definitive instance of retrieving information from memory.

What you are practicing is the recall itself—not the exposure. You are rehearsing the act of going into your memory banks and digging around until you find what you're looking for.

If you depend heavily on highlighting and re-reading? All you're reinforcing is your ability to highlight and re-read!

Imagine you're studying for a professional qualification. Here's how effective, active spaced recall might look:

Day 1: You work through the material for the first time.

Day 2: You convert your notes into flashcards and diagrams. You practice recalling these, sorting the cards into piles according to how easily you can recall them.

Day 4: You return to your flashcards, paying most attention to the difficult pile.

Day 8: You return again, and do the same. You notice what you've remembered and what you've forgotten, and adjust accordingly. Gradually, the difficult pile grows smaller. You continue until you feel familiar with the material and can recall all of it with ease (how long this takes will vary).

Spaced repetition is best when it's *intelligent*.

Ask yourself: "What are my memory gaps?" Then focus on those.

Keep **self-testing** and **drilling the weakest points**. Then **repeat**.

Remember that reading and re-reading achieves little. The thing you want to practice is *recall*. That means relying solely on your memory to call up an idea or concept. Close your books, explain in your own words what you've just read, re-create a diagram from memory, or write out a process in order without consulting any outside resources.

Break Learning into Short Sessions Over Time

Perhaps you noticed something interesting about the "Remembering Curve."

Every *instance* of recall boosted memory back up to 100%. It does not matter how long that instance is!

This means that while prolonged study marathons may feel like they're working, they still only count as *one* instance of repetition—and wear you out in the process.

How do we maximize the effect of spaced repetition while reducing cognitive fatigue?

That's easy: **Shorter, more frequent review sessions.**

Spaced repetition works because it provides an opportunity for the brain to consolidate. The *frequency* matters more than the *duration* or *intensity*.

A grueling three-hour study session on day 1, 3, and 6 may get you precisely the same results as three targeted 20-minute review sessions.

The former, however, will take you three times as long and risks burning you out. This wouldn't be so bad were it not for the fact that cognitive fatigue actually undermines your memory, so you may be spending more time to get more tired... and still have worse recall.

There's no need to overload your brain. Just keep things current.

You can change up the format of your review as well. For example, if you're learning a language:

- Spend 10 minutes on a language app each morning to run through vocabulary drills
- Listen for 10 minutes on the weekends to an audiobook or podcast in your target language, and then challenge yourself to use your new vocabulary words to make a summary of what you've heard
- Once a week, sit down and see if you can draw a mind map of everything you've absorbed in the last seven days, devise a little speech, or jot down some questions or ideas that you'd like to revise next.

Slow, consistent exposure to newly acquired information gives your brain time to absorb and consolidate without rush and overwhelm.

Keep reminding yourself that the memory is a little like a battery that will lose its charge over time… unless you recharge it. Spaced repetition is like recharging your memory by reinforcing new knowledge and understanding.

Mix It Up and Spread It Out: How Interleaving Builds Smarter, Long-Term Learning

"As we use our memories, the things we recall become more recallable. Things in competition with the memories become less recallable."

- Robert Bjork

Every skill we want to learn is really made up of smaller skills. It makes sense then to break things down, master each chunk separately, then combine everything.

However, many of us unwittingly stop just short of the "combine everything" step and get stuck for far too long in the "one skill at a time" zone. In real life, however, we usually use all of our skills at once.

If we want our mastery to be flexible, adaptive, and contextual, then our practice has to reflect this. Enter interleaving.

Interleaving = The evidence-backed technique of structuring your practice/study around mixed combinations of related concepts, rather than single concepts at a time.

What's the benefit? With practice that is interleaved, you store information more deeply, retrieve it more reliably, and allow your brain to build essential patterns and *connections between concepts.*

"Blocked practice" or "massed practice" (one-at-a-time learning in sequential chunks) is also useful, but it doesn't challenge your brain to actively pull together everything it's learned and find new strategies to solve unfamiliar challenges and problems.

A good balance is beginning with blocked practice, then increasingly use interleaving to acquire mastery.

Along with spaced repetition, interleaving is one of the most extensively studied and evidenced techniques for creating deep comprehension and lasting retention (Firth et. al., 2021; Yan & Sana, 2021; Samani & Pan, 2021). Used *together*, they are a powerhouse.

For many students, the idea of interleaving seems trivial at first, but try it for a period and the effects will be *very* evident:

- You improve your mental flexibility
- You enhance your ability to transfer skills to other areas
- You become a more creative problem solver
- You gain confidence
- You create more secure long-term memories

By constantly asking your brain to **retrieve, compare, reinforce, and apply knowledge in various settings and across various activities**

over time, your learning becomes rich and three dimensional.

Mix Tasks Into Your Daily Study or Work Routine

In school, were you indoctrinated into the "one hour per topic" dogma?

It goes like this: One study session = one subject.

So, first is math, then chemistry, then English Lit. And in each of those hours, you focus on just one topic at a time—one day in math class you learn long division, the next you learn multiplication.

With the interleaving approach, you **mix things up.** For example, math class might include working on problems from all different chapters in the textbook—multiplication, division, fractions, and more. Or you may only work on fractions, but switch up the *kinds* of problems you tackle, and change the format of the practice questions.

Instead of: AAAAA BBBBB CCCCC DDDDD

You have: AAACD BDACA DDCBB BABCAC

If you are busy in the middle of an "A" block, your brain gets lazy—it knows that its next task is "A" and so it relies on short- instead of long-term memory. It gets complacent. You learn less.

On the other hand, every time you switch, you ask your brain to actively recall previous information. You are challenged to find connections between activities. You are forced to carefully consider your problem-solving approaches, not merely using a technique because that's what you're doing that day.

This enhances your memory.

It keeps you on your toes.

Interleaving your daily practice is fairly straightforward.

1. **Break your session into smaller chunks**
2. **Rotate between these chunks so you are never doing the same thing twice in a row**

So, if you're learning from a chemistry textbook, spend your study hour mixing up exercises and tasks from four different chapters, or tackle the same chapter but in multiple ways—one essay question, a few short-form answers, some multiple-choice quizzes...

You can also add variety in the format of your materials. For example, instead of slogging away reading one chapter in the textbook, you could:

- Spend 20 minutes watching a video about Chapter 3, taking notes

- Spend 20 minutes making a mind map or flash cards for Chapter 4
- Spend 20 minutes doing a practice test paper for Chapter 5, asking a friend to grade you

You're working on the same topic, but taking different perspectives on it, activating a deeper grasp of broader patterns and relationships. There are countless ways to slice and dice your material; all that matters is that you're keeping limber and cognitively flexible as you switch between tasks.

Once you get the hang of interleaved practice, you may notice that

- It's a little more challenging and engaging
- Time seems to go a lot quicker
- You learn more!

With interleaving practice, you often work harder, but you prevent the learning fatigue that comes from dull repetition.

Research into the effects of interleaving has been encouraging, with most finding that recall and retention is drastically improved when material is interleaved rather than blocked (Roher, 2012; 2013).

Furthermore, a research review of a whopping 254 studies found that on average, people were able to recall around 10% more information when using spaced repetition, compared to "massed practice" (Cepeda et. al. , 2006, *Distributed Practice in Verbal Recall Tasks: A Review and Quantitative Synthesis).*

Can you imagine how effective the two might be when combined?

Spread Learning Sessions Across Your Week

Cramming is a terrible habit. Your exhaustion and panic may give the illusion that something is changing for you. In truth, a brain that is depleted and overstressed is a brain that cannot process, consolidate, or retain information effectively.

Combine spaced repetition with interleaving by evenly spreading out your work over the course of a week.

Break that exhausting study marathon down into 20- or 30-minute chunks, then evenly distribute those chunks across your calendar, remembering to mix things up so you're not spending too long on any one topic, approach, or activity.

Cramming gives the illusion of productivity, but spacing your learning helps your brain *consolidate* that knowledge into long-term memory. Instead of doing one marathon session, break your learning into 15–30-minute chunks spread across the week.

Spaced, interleaved practice is not just more effective. It also allows you to squeeze in personal development projects around your existing commitments, making gains even though your schedule only has small pockets of time here and there.

Instead of wearing yourself out with two straight hours of French practice on a Sunday afternoon, for example, try this:

- **Monday:** 15 minutes of new vocabulary (e.g., travel words)
- **Tuesday:** 15 minutes drilling vocabulary flashcards
- **Wednesday:** 25 minutes practicing a conversation exercise online with a fellow student
- **Thursday:** 15 minutes reviewing and revising, plus a vocabulary quiz

The spaced repetition means you're far less likely to slide down that Forgetting Curve, and—did you notice?—you can often get away with investing far less study time overall because you are utilizing the time you have so much more efficiently.

Build in Quick Reviews of Past Material

One of the reasons interleaving works so well is that it encourages the brain to engage in active recall. Each attempted recall has to be new—you cannot fall back on short-term memory or momentum.

No shortcuts.

No assumptions.

For example, you can't look at a math problem and think, "Oh, I have to solve this in XYZ way because today is XYZ day, and I'm doing an XYZ exercise, so I'll just do what I did for the last question…"

Instead, you have to ask, "What kind of problem is this? What is the question asking me? Have I seen this kind of thing before? What tools do I have?"

You can encourage this kind of deliberate, flexible thinking by spending the first few minutes of every session reviewing prior material.

- Quickly summarize, in a sentence or two, what you covered in the last session.
- Quickly scan over your notes to refresh your memory, whether they're summaries, mind maps, flashcards, or diagrams.

- Do a quick five question quiz.
- Without consulting your notes at all, try to see how much of the last session you can recall from memory alone. Notice the gaps!
- If you're learning a particular athletic, musical, or creative skill, quickly drill it start to finish. Run through a guitar piece or quickly rehearse the last part of a speech.

Task-Switching: Refresh Focus With Cognitive Micro-Breaks

"The secret of happiness is variety, but the secret of variety, like the secret of all spices, is knowing when to use it."

- **Daniel Gilbert**

We all know that distraction is bad and that we need to avoid the dreaded multitasking.

But what if there was such a thing as **intentional distraction**?

If you're exercising, you know what it's like to completely fatigue a muscle. You work and work, and eventually you exhaust that muscle and can get nothing more out of it. Your only options?

- Take a break
- Train a different muscle

It's the same with your brain, which can get depleted and worn out just like any muscle in your body. If you're on the other end of hours of intense cognitive effort, you may feel stuck. Exhausted. Blocked.

This is a sign that **you need a cognitive reset**. You have the same two options:

- Take a break
- Switch to a different cognitive task

This *intentional* distraction is not about wasting time scrolling or stressing yourself out on social media.

It's about **switching to a lighter, unrelated mental activity that essentially "flushes" your brain's working memory** and gives you a chance to quickly reboot your focus and attention.

These light, relatively undemanding tasks allow you to disengage and refresh, but without completely pausing to rest. It's the equivalent of switching to an easy arm exercise when you've fatigued your leg muscles, for example.

Even a few minutes of this kind of "sideways rest" can boost performance, enhance your focus, and increase your stamina in the long term.

Change the channel.

- If you're doing something mentally demanding, briefly switch to a purely physical activity for a while, and vice versa.
- If you've been plugging away in isolation for hours, reach out for a chat with a friend or call someone.
- If you've been staring at images and diagrams all day, take a break by reading some fun and lighthearted fiction.

There's no need to power through tiredness and burn yourself out. Take a productive "break" and give yourself a chance to catch your breath and renew your clarity and focus.

Einstein was known to take regular breaks to play violin. Surrealist painter Salvadore Dali would take the briefest naps. Bach would go for a short walk out in the fresh air, amongst the trees. What would work for you?

Use Cognitive Puzzles Between Study Blocks

- Do a simple puzzle
- Sketch a doodle
- Play a word game
- Solve a basic logic puzzle, like Sudoku
- Do an easy crossword

- Solve a low-level brainteaser
- Play a simple matching game

Your performance on these puzzles and games doesn't matter—what's important is that you're giving your brain the opportunity to switch gears. You hit the reset button on your short-term memory, and get your brain prepared for the next round.

Tip: Puzzles change your internal context, but you can switch your external context, too. Literally get up and move around, change your seat, vary your posture or position, or experiment with a few stretches to wake up different parts of your body.

Alternate with Creative or Sensory Tasks

Imagine that all activities fall into several broad categories:

- Creative
- Sensory
- Physical
- Analytical
- Social
- Practical/Administrative

You don't necessarily have to *stop* to have a break. You can give yourself a rest simply by switching from one broad activity type to another.

If you're designing a poster layout (creative), for example, take a break by doing a number puzzle (analytical) or make a To Do list for the following day (practical).

If you're working hard on your golf swing (physical), take a break by chatting with a friend (social), or enjoying a delicious snack break (sensory).

The idea is to switch your focus, so that your overloaded short memory circuits have a moment to cool down and refresh.

Tip: With a little forethought, you can schedule your time so that your breaks are essentially tasks that are also valuable to you in reaching other goals. You can work on your programming skills, take "breaks" to practice your sketching, and in the spare scraps of time you can squeeze in household chores and other errands.

Your brain is resting throughout, despite being constantly active. This is **creative, opportunistic interleaving**!

Set a Timer to Prevent Drift

Switching tasks *before* you're truly fatigued is not intentional distraction. It's just distraction.

Truly beneficial cognitive resets will be:

- **Short**—a 2-5 minute "micro-break" is plenty.
- **Intentional**—*you* decide when they happen.
- **Strategic**—you decide *how* they happen.

It goes without saying, but getting passively drawn down paths chosen for you by social media algorithms is not likely to recharge you. Neither is grabbing hold of a convenient distraction and letting it pull you off course.

You want to be energized, not derailed.

- Do you notice your cognitive performance dipping a little? Are you slowing down or finding things more confusing?
- Are you feeling irritable, resentful, bored, frustrated, or overwhelmed?
- Are you making more careless mistakes?
- Are you feeling like your mind is wandering and you are more distractable?
- Are you *physically* drained—sore eyes, headache, or aching muscles?

All of these are potential signs that you're cognitively depleted. You may need to rest or switch gears.

Summary

- Vygotsky's **Zone of Proximal Development (ZPD)** refers to the range of activities that a person can achieve with help and support from a more knowledgeable other. It's where learning actually happens. These "developmental training wheels" help us scaffold new learning on existing social knowledge.
- Stay just outside of your comfort zone. **Observe, mimic, and eventually internalize** the more knowledgeable other's mastery as your own. Remember that external dialogue becomes internal thought process, so use peer learning and instructional scaffolding to bootstrap your own understanding.
- **Spaced repetition is a proven way to combat the Forgetting Curve** and reinforce retention. **Actively review** things before you have the chance to forget them. Use shorter, more frequent review sessions.
- **Interleaving** means structuring your practice/study around mixed

combinations of related concepts, rather than single concepts at a time.
- **Combine spaced repetition with interleaving** by evenly spreading out your work over the course of a week.
- Task switching is **intentional distraction** that can act as a cognitive refresh. Switch to a lighter, unrelated mental activity to flush your brain's working memory and give you a chance to reset.
- **A "sideways break" could include easy cognitive puzzles, creative activities, or sensory tasks**—but set a timer to prevent unhelpful distraction and attentional drift.

Chapter 3: Stay in the Goldilocks Zone

Learn Like You're Playing a Video Game—Unlock Deep Learning by Gamifying Your Process

"The game of life is worth playing, but the struggle is the prize."

- **William Ralph Inge**

Earlier, in our chapter about Vygotsky and the ZPD, we touched on certain characteristics of the deep learning flow state. The activities most associated with real development and learning all have:

- Clear goals and milestones
- Immediate feedback
- The chance for self-instruction
- Peer learning and progressive modeling
- Increasing intensity and iterative learning

It doesn't take a brain surgeon to see the overlap—**could *gaming* be a form of deep work or flow?**

Researchers using data from the Adolescent Brain Cognitive Development (ABCD) Study asked a very similar question (see abcdstudy.org). To answer it, they looked at almost 2000 children of 9 to 10 years of age, finding that those who played video games more than three hours per day performed better on impulse control and working memory tests than those who never played.

According to National Institute on Drug Abuse (NIDA) Director Nora Volkow,

> "This study adds to our growing understanding of the associations between playing video games and brain development [...] Numerous studies have linked video gaming to behavior and mental health problems. This study suggests that there may also be cognitive benefits associated with this popular pastime, which are worthy of further investigation."

Research is still being done on exactly what happens in the brain during gaming, but the researchers found definitive differences in speed and accuracy in the gaming group. Brain scans revealed heightened activity in areas of the brain associated with attention and memory, but, interestingly, less brain activity in areas related to vision.

Does this mean we should all acquire a gaming addiction and squeeze in as many hours a day as possible?

Nope—an updated version of the research paper explains clearly that gaming is also associated with:

- Depression
- ADHD symptoms
- Anxiety

What's more, as we all know, correlation does not equal causation; the study could have merely discovered that children who are better at certain cognitive tasks naturally gravitate towards activities that rely on those skills.

Nevertheless, the study and others like it pose interesting questions.

Related studies done at Caltech involve creating AI models and then studying those as simulations of human cognitive processes (Logan et. al., 2012, *Using deep reinforcement learning to reveal how the brain encodes abstract state-space representations in high-dimensional environments*).

The researchers find that playing video games well means knowing how to:

- **Observe**—Take in enormous amounts of data

- **Filter**—Quickly decide what is relevant to the main task and what isn't
- **Act**—Make conscious, strategic decisions

Whether you are driving a car, performing a violin recital, or doing open heart surgery, your brain needs to be *switched on*—taking everything in, filtering it, and acting on only those things are important.

Video games may mimic this kind of immersive, complex real-world environment, and challenge us to cultivate more focused decision making. It's not that video games themselves are beneficial, but rather that **the skills they cultivate in us may be extremely transferrable.**

We all live in the real world, which is messy, complicated, and sometimes moving quite quickly.

There's a lot of noise and distraction.

If we hope to develop the capacity for deep learning, we need to practice with exercises that are:

- Active
- Fully immersive
- Complex and real

Video games, far from being mere entertainment or distraction, can be harnessed as **interactive learning platforms that cultivate problem-**

solving, critical thinking, attention control, and adaptability.

There are two insights here:

1. To the extent that video games strengthen working memory attention, impulse control etc., they improve our deep learning capacity.
2. To the extent that any of our learning activities resemble games, they stimulate working memory attention, impulse control, etc.

But not all games are created equal!

Pick games that challenge your ability to manage resources, strategize, solve problems, adapt, and filter out distractions… under time pressure. Remember the principles of flow and choose activities that are not too easy but not impossibly hard. The right game will adjust with you, encouraging you to adapt, track evolving patterns, and adjust on the fly.

To make gaming a deliberate learning practice, ask: **"What specific skills do I want to develop?"**

Then choose a game that will sharpen those skills.

Now, it's no longer a "game"—it's a mental gym.

After a gaming session, pause to reflect not on your performance, but on the strategies you applied, why, and what you're learning.

- Did I allocate my resources well?
- Did I succeed in juggling priorities?
- Did I successfully pivot when circumstances changed?
- Did I anticipate changes and adapt to them?

Not only will this kind of questioning help you mine the gaming experience for real-world insight, but you will also be developing your *metacognition*.

Let's take a closer look at how to apply both games and gamification principles to our own deliberate learning practice.

Practice Focused Attention by Filtering Out Irrelevant Information

Much of the cognitive benefit of gaming arises from improvements to single-mindedness, or focused vision on the task at hand and *only* that task.

In other words, **productive tunnel vision**.

In every task—video games or real life—your brain works hard to filter through a flood of sensory information, only a tiny fraction of which is actually necessary for the task at hand.

It may seem counterintuitive, but a big part of your cognitive load is managing all the stuff you have to *actively ignore* in your field of awareness!

There is no task that doesn't benefit from this kind of focused attention and single-mindedness.

If you're struggling with distractibility and shallow engagement, how can you improve? The answer is: Deliberately include your own intentional focus exercises into your everyday life.

- While going for a walk, set yourself a challenge to only notice certain stimuli and filter out the rest. For example, zoom in on number plates, traffic light signals, or road markings, but tune out people, weather, and what's happening on the ground (the exact stimuli are arbitrary; you can just as easily reverse this order).
- Play puzzle and strategy games that require quick responses to visual cues—the time will force your brain to quickly home in on what matters, and filter out the rest to make a decision.
- Whenever a new task comes your way, get into the habit of immediately asking, "What's the single most important thing

here?" Always look for the key information and the main goal.

Strengthen Working Memory With Challenging Cognitive Tasks

The 9- to 10-year-olds who played three or more hours of games a day were not only better at impulse control (read, focused attention and single-mindedness), they also demonstrated better memory.

This makes sense. Many games require that we keep a mental tab on several bits of open information, holding and manipulating certain facts and details in the short term to solve problems. You remember a trick, a character, or an area of the map that may be relevant for solving the current dilemma, and you quickly retrieve that data and apply it in the present.

What kind of games build working memory?

- Jigsaw puzzles , sudoku, chess, checkers, and all manner of card games are easy low-tech options.
- You can also try digital memory-boosting games and apps like Lumosity or Elevate.
- Find everyday ways to challenge your memory—see if you can remember a string of spoken directions for reaching a

certain destination, challenge yourself to recall one important detail from every conversation you have, or get into the habit of reading multi-step instructions *once*, memorizing them and doing the task from memory.

Improve Impulse Control Through Fast-Paced Decision Games

In this context, impulse control refers to the ability to resist immediate desires and urges, and instead force yourself to **pause, think carefully, and act with self-control and conscious deliberation.**

Impulse control is about emotional regulation and the ability to withstand delayed gratification in the service of a goal.

How can we cultivate stronger impulse control?

- Play games that require patience and deliberation, like chess or war games where the consequences of strategy play out over many turns.
- On the other hand, you can also strengthen your self-control by engaging in games that are so fast paced you simply don't have time to dawdle and entertain distractions! Short bursts of

intense first-person shooter games or anything that requires a rapid response will strengthen your impulse control.
- Be self-aware and continually adjust. If you notice yourself veering outside a comfortable emotional zone, stop. Just pause for a moment and take a breath. Choose your next move *from that stillness*, rather than being reactive and emotional.

In a way, all of life is a strategy game.

We have objectives (some of them really hard!) and we are often thrown into things without a tutorial or a practice round.

It's easy to engage in artificial learning activities if they are simple and done on our own terms. Real life, however, contains a lot more ambiguity, urgency, and complexity. Stress and a lack of clarity are not abnormalities, but a part of the game.

Pause and center yourself.

Talk yourself through:

- "Wait, what is my goal again? What am I trying to achieve here?"
- "What am I struggling with? Who can teach me or show me? *How* can I learn to do this?"
- "How did I solve the last problem that looked a bit like this?"

- "What do I have? What do I need? Why isn't this working? What will?"
- "Let me try X and see what happens. I'll use that feedback and adjust myself."

When you are gaming/living this way, you are *learning to learn.*

Challenge, ambiguity, and time limits can be stressful, yes. But there is fun and learning in it, too. Can you find it?

Consider all possible outcomes, weigh up your decisions, and act—**the game is about letting the process shape and refine you over time.**

Cognitive Load Management: Lighten the Mental Load to Unlock Deep Learning

"It's not the load that breaks you down, it's the way you carry it."

- **Lena Horne**

We know that we need to stay in the **flow zone**.

We also know that for deep learning to occur, we need to be inside our ZPD—**Zone of Proximal Development**.

- Csikszentmihalyi's flow model is about the optimal range for *focused attention and absorption.*
- Vygotsky's model is about the optimal range for *development and learning.*
- In this chapter, we'll look at a similar principle but through psychologist John Sweller's model, which is about the optimal range for *cognitive effort.*

In essence, these are not really different theories, but the same underlying concept seen through different lenses.

The underlying concept? **Optimal performance is about being in the optimal range.**

Sweller's cognitive load theory (*Sweller, 1988.* "Cognitive load during problem solving: Effects on learning". *Cognitive Science*) begins with the fact that **the brain's cognitive powers are limited**—something that's easy to forget in our endless hustle-and-productivity culture!

Working memory is like the surface of a table: We can lay out a few things on the table and get to work, but the tabletop is fixed in its dimensions. Put too many things on the table? Stuff falls off. Stress and chaos. Productivity *drops*.

Our working memory is the same. It too has fixed dimensions and suffers when overloaded.

Forgetting things?

Feeling stressed and overwhelmed?

You might be disrespecting your brain's natural limitations.

Some cognitive psychologists set the limit at a mere handful of ideas—just seven or so!—that can be held in the working memory at any one time (see the famous *The Magical Number Seven, Plus or Minus Two: Some Limits on Our Capacity for Processing Information* by George A. Miller, 1956).

It's the same idea again: Our brain is built to handle a certain cognitive load, but that capacity is not infinite. Beyond a certain point, cognition suffers.

Not all cognitive load is the same:

- **Intrinsic Load:** A task's inherent difficulty; i.e., how challenging, large, or complex it is.
    - Brushing your teeth = low intrinsic cognitive load
    - Writing an entire screenplay in three days = high intrinsic load
- **Extraneous Load:** Cognitive demands arising not from the task itself but from the environment; i.e., additional impediments and distractions. For example:
    - A fly buzzing around your head while you're trying to focus

- A teacher with a hard-to-understand accent
- A cluttered desk
- Outdated learning materials in a format you dislike
- Physical discomfort
- **Germane Load:** The mental effort you make to form helpful new connections, schemas, or mental frameworks. Germane load is effortful, but improves learning in the long run.
  - Actively connecting what you already know to the new things you're learning
  - Creating helpful mind maps, visual aids, mnemonics, diagrams, etc.
  - Using analogies, stories, or metaphors to bridge your understanding to an unfamiliar topic

Cognitive load is multidimensional, meaning the demand comes from many different directions. For example, even an "easy" task will feel difficult if we're in a highly distracting environment (like trying to read a book during a metal concert) and an extremely difficult task can be achieved if we have enough time and the right learning tools to digest it.

Parsing Sweller's theory down, we discover **four main goals** with respect to optimizing our cognition:

Goal 1: Stay comfortably within our optimal cognitive range, i.e. neither under- nor overloading our capacity.

Goal 2: *Manage* intrinsic load—find ways to work around a task's inbuilt challenge.

Goal 3: *Minimize* extraneous load—cut down as much as possible on noise, distractions, and irrelevancies.

Goal 4: *Maximize* germane load—do what we can to use tools to help us process, absorb, and retain what we're learning.

Deliberate, masterful learners understand **the art of self-regulation**. They are self-aware and know when they are outside their optimal range.

Anyone can notice that they're not performing very well on a learning task, but it takes a little something extra to know *why* you feel that way, and what to do to correct the situation.

First things first:

- Being cognitively overwhelmed is not a sign of stupidity or laziness.
- Feeling depleted doesn't mean you lack passion or discipline.
- Running out of steam doesn't mean that something's going wrong, or that you

need to drastically change up your process.

There's no need to beat yourself up if you discover your cognitive performance dipping—read it as a neutral sign and simply adjust.

Here are some signs you're simply asking too much of your brain:

- You're struggling to comprehend certain things; feeling confused
- Emotionally, you're stressed and frustrated
- You're falling back on old habits and finding it hard to be creative
- You're not holding onto things; you're more forgetful
- Your performance is dropping; you're losing accuracy, speed, power, etc.

Instead of asking yourself, "How I can do more? How can I power through?" ask, **"How can I reduce cognitive load right now?"**

Below are some useful practical ideas.

Chunk and Sequence Information to Reduce Overwhelm

Goal: Manage intrinsic load

Imagine that your long-term memory is a giant open field with plenty of space to store learned information. The catch is that the only way to access this giant field is through a teeny, tiny hole in a fence.

There's enough space in the field for a big, difficult concept... but how are you going to get it through that teeny tiny hole in the fence?

Answer: Cut it up!

Difficult tasks are always going to be difficult—we can't change that fact. What we *can* do is break those tasks down into smaller chunks that we can process one step at a time. This reduces intrinsic cognitive load.

"Chunking" is the name given to this breaking down process.

- **Always be simplifying**—if you encounter a challenging formula, sentence, or concept, break it down. Number by number. Word by word. Just try to understand one piece at a time, then move on to the next, as though you were taking small bites.
- **Use pictures, diagrams, and mind maps**—a picture paints a thousand words. Condense information in one place and experiment with representing concepts in a visual rather than verbal way.

- **Use analogy and metaphor**—what is the new concept like? How does it connect to something you're already familiar with?
- **Make it real**—experiential learning is more memorable. Find ways to get hands on and try things out for yourself if possible. You may gain new insight and understanding by being out there in the field.
- **Tell stories**—human beings find it easier to understand and care about narratives they're emotionally invested in, so craft stories that bring abstract ideas to life. Connect concepts directly to yourself and find the deeper meaning and context.

As an example, if you're studying for a history exam, don't get intimidated by the whole syllabus. Just take it steady with one section at a time—if a chunk *still* feels overwhelming, then just break it down further.

Don't be alarmed if some material is tricky; if you feel stuck, eliminate the lowest hanging fruit first. Change up the material format, take a mini-break, or play around with interleaving.

If the task feels more *psychologically* manageable, it's likely to also be more *cognitively* manageable.

Eliminate Distractions and Simplify Your Learning Environment

Goal: Minimize extraneous load

It is not just your internal environment that matters in learning, but your external environment, too.

Your physical environment reflects and influences your mental state, including your ability to carry a mental load:

- Clutter
- Distractions
- Interruptions
- Temptations
- Discomforts
- Noise

If you are experiencing a lot of mental distraction, it may be because you are in an environment with high extraneous load.

Your desk is messy.

There's noise outside and your phone pings every five minutes.

You're cold and you're annoyed by that one broken letter on your keyboard and you have four other browser tabs open and there's something delicious in the kitchen you keep thinking about...

Outer clutter and noise are usually continuous with inner clutter and noise. Reduce one and you reduce the other.

All of this eats up mental bandwidth while giving you nothing in return. The only solution is to reduce it as much as possible:

- Clear your desk of everything except the materials you're currently using.
- Silence notifications or remove phones and devices completely.
- Use apps and tools to block access to time-wasting sites, streamline your desktop, and cut down on digital distraction.
- Alert everyone that you're busy and not to be disturbed. Set boundaries and protect them.
- Make sure your workspace is calm, well-lit, and at the right temperature. Think comfort, not luxury.
- Have all your tools and materials organized, within reach, and in good working order.
- Rewrite instructions to be simple and clear, and try to trim away extraneous information by paraphrasing or summarizing.
- Use tools and apps to streamline your work process and give you less to worry about (naturally, be mindful that these

tools and apps are themselves not becoming a source of distraction!).
- Be mindful of your attitude—create a positive mental environment by staying open, curious, and optimistic, rather than approaching learning tasks with dread and resentment.
- Mentally prepare yourself with a little ritual to mark the beginning of a study session. Light a candle, do a few minutes of visualization or meditation, or scribble random worries in a journal to tackle later.

Link New Knowledge to What You Already Know

Goal: Maximize germane load

As they say, don't work harder, work smarter. Any learning activity is going to take time, effort, and energy, so think carefully about where you'd like to invest these limited resources.

Instead of working hard to build something from scratch, piggyback off of something that's already been built.

Learning is not just additive; i.e., you keep dumping new facts and information onto the pile of existing facts in your brain. Instead, **the sum total of your knowledge is arranged like**

a web—everything connects meaningfully to everything else.

To make new learning last, you need to actively wire it into this web:

- **Review**. Before you even start, quickly brainstorm what you already know about a topic—it's often more than you think, so activate those pre-existing links.
- **Connect the new thing to old things**. What is this new concept most like? Where does it fit? How? Actively seek out those links and connections.
- **Continually change formats**. Express the same idea visually, verbally, diagrammatically, etc. See an idea from as many different angles as possible.
- **Use the "Feynman Technique"** (more on this later). Regularly pause to explain out loud to yourself what you've just learned, in your own words.
- **Reflect** on what you're learning, and how it compares to your approach historically. In what ways is this new challenge similar to previous ones? In what ways is it different?

Balancing Stress for Better Learning: What the Yerkes-Dodson Curve Teaches Us

"When we long for life without difficulties, remind us that oaks grow strong in contrary winds and diamonds are made under pressure."

- **Peter Marshall**

The final Goldilocks zone we'll consider in this chapter is the optimal zone for *stress*.

It may seem strange to ask, "What is the ideal amount of stress?"

Aren't we supposed to be reducing stress at all costs?

Maybe not.

The curve proposed by Robert Yerkes and John Dodson offers a similar insight to the one we've gleaned from Csikszentmihalyi, Vygotsky and Sweller: When it comes to optimal performance, **extremes are undesirable**; instead, it's that sweet spot in the middle where the magic happens.

The Yerkes-Dodson Curve tells us that **a moderate level of stress can enhance performance, while too little or too much can hinder it.**

In 1908, Yerkes and Dodson's research led them to propose that as stress (or "physiological arousal") increases, performance quality increases, but then drops again, i.e. it falls on a bell curve with the highest performance somewhere in the middle.

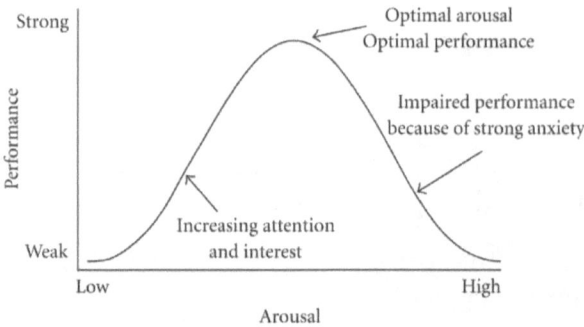

Yerkes and Dodson, Hebbian - Diamond DM, et al. (2007). "The Temporal Dynamics Model of Emotional Memory Processing: A Synthesis on the Neurobiological Basis of Stress-Induced Amnesia, Flashbulb and Traumatic Memories, and the Yerkes-Dodson Law". Neural Plasticity: 33. doi:10.1155/2007/60803.

While it makes sense that too much stress is a problem, it can be harder to wrap your head around the idea that being ultra-calm, relaxed, and at ease is *also* a sub-optimal state!

Big caveat: The original study by Yerkes and Dodson has since come under fire for methodological flaws. Being originally conducted on mice and not people, the results have also never been replicated.

Nevertheless, the now-classic graph still holds value as a practical guide for recognizing a generally sound principle: **If you can identify and inhabit your optimal arousal zone, you can maximize focus, creativity, and retention.** In other words, you can improve deep learning.

Let's look at how.

Find Your Personal Peak Zone: Not Too Calm, Not Too Stressed

A few things to keep in mind about the "optimal stress zone":

- **It's subjective**. Two people may have very different perceptions of the same situation.
- **It's dynamic.** Your sensitivity and resilience will vary over time, so that your perception of stress today may not be the same as it was yesterday.
- **It's dependent on context.** Your stress zone will not be the same across tasks—some activities, environments, and circumstances may be madly stressful, while others have you barely breaking a sweat.

How is it possible to identify the *ideal* stress range, if there are so many variables?

The answer is **self-awareness + metacognition.**

Constantly tune into your own internal signals (awareness), then adjust yourself accordingly (metacognition).

Moment by moment, notice not just the quantity of your output, but the quality.

How do you feel?

What's the nature of your conscious awareness?

How is your brain working right now?

"Stress" is multifactorial. When you think of it more broadly as "arousal" you can learn to read the signals that your body, heart, and mind are sending.

Here are some signs that you're experiencing too much stress:

- Physical signs: Muscles tightness, dizziness, headaches, jaw tension, racing heart, and shallow, constricted breathing.
- Mental signs: Racing, disorganized thoughts, forgetfulness, feeling like nothing is sinking in, and confusion.
- Emotional signs: Feelings of panic, overwhelm, fear, anxiety, resignation, and resentment.

Sensations do not have to be dramatic to warrant your attention. In fact, the better you become at reading these subtle changes, the more *micro-course corrections* you can make along the way, and the smoother your overall learning journey will be.

For example, you may have started on a new section of work and quickly notice that your shoulders are suddenly tightening a tiny bit, and your thoughts have taken a small turn towards the pessimistic. What now?

Here are some ways to reduce overall arousal and bring you back into the optimal range.

- **Consider lowering cognitive load.** Ask yourself whether your biggest reduction will be in intrinsic, extrinsic, or germane load. Where is most of your stress coming from right now?
  - **Intrinsic load too high**? Chunk the task down, simplify or use visual aids and metaphors to start chipping away at the block.
  - **Extrinsic load too high**? Identify and remove distractions and noise. Switch up your environment or change your materials.
  - **What about germane load**? Ask if there is some tool to help bootstrap your understanding that you're not using. Try to build a temporary scaffold. Ask for help.
- **Have a cognitive reset.** Leave the task alone and switch your brain to something completely different for a few minutes, then return with fresh eyes.

- **Take a complete break.** Sometimes, a small cognitive reset is not enough, and you need a bigger rest. Have a nap or a leisurely bath, take a long walk in nature, enjoy a hobby, or socialize with friends until your nervous system reorganizes.
- **Do an attitude check.** Finally, consider that your sense of exhaustion and overwhelm may be purely psychological. Take a look at your self-talk and ask whether you're being overly pessimistic or putting unnecessarily high demands on yourself. Sometimes, when we change the attitude we take to tasks, they seem far, far less stressful.
  - For example, instead of "I have to write this enormous essay," tell yourself, "I just have to get started, and it doesn't have to be perfect immediately."

On the other hand, you may not be stressed *enough*.

In all the corporate stress management literature out there, you will struggle to find advice on how to *increase* your stress levels. But often, this is precisely what we need to do to boost our motivation, productivity, and sense of accomplishment.

One problem? We can sometimes confuse the symptoms of over-stress and under-stress.

We may be feeling lethargic, uninspired, or bored, and mistakenly assume that this means we're burning out and need a break. We may need precisely the opposite!

Here are some signs you may be experiencing too little stress:

- Physical signs: Feelings of heaviness and inertia, tiredness, slouching, and sleepiness.
- Mental signs: A wandering, distractable mind.
- Emotional signs: Boredom.

Here are some ways to mindfully increase overall arousal so you're more squarely in that generative, deep work zone:

- **Consider increasing cognitive load.** If we hope to actively learn and improve, we need to increase difficulty level as our mastery improves. It's easy to get complacent and stall at a certain level. Ask yourself where you may be coasting:
  - **Intrinsic load too low?** Level up—it doesn't have to be a big jump, just challenge yourself to do something unfamiliar. Try combining existing skills or broadening their application.
  - **Extrinsic load too low?** Usually, we want extrinsic load to be as low as possible, but it's worth asking if your learning exercises are overly simplified. Try to make them more reflective of real life. Here, strategically

chosen video games can be extremely useful, as can sitting in a busy coffee shop to work.
- **What about germane load**? You may have become too comfortable with a familiar format of your practice exercise or task. Mix things up. Throw a spanner in the works and challenge yourself to adapt. Take those training wheels off!

- **Set a more audacious goal.** Sometimes, playing it safe can be the most boring, uninspiring thing you can do. When the goal is too easily acquired, we can lose interest and motivation. Instead, put on a little more pressure. Give yourself a tight deadline. Imagine the most you can do and then set yourself a goal 1% bigger than that. Find ways to push yourself:
  - If you're used to a 20-minute work window, extend it to 25 minutes
  - Set up mini competitions with yourself ("How many flashcards can I cover in 10 minutes? More than last time?")

- **Do an attitude check.** "I'm bored" can be secret code for something else.
  - "I don't actually want to do this."
  - "This doesn't really need to be done and deep down I know it."
  - "I want this, but I'm actually not convinced I'm on the right path."

  > Fatigue and disinterest could be warning signs that you've lost a sense of purpose

and need to check in again with your values.

Match Task Difficulty to Your Stress Level

Bearing in mind that stress is **subjective, dynamic,** and **context-dependent**, pay attention to the state of mind you adopt for different types of activities.

In general, simple and straightforward tasks tend to benefit from higher stress levels, while more complex, important tasks usually require peace and quiet to tackle successfully.

For more challenging, complex, or important tasks, a conventional stress management protocol is ideal.

For simple tasks, play around with *increasing* stress.

What's a simple task? That's for you to decide, but it could be:

- Quickly proofreading a long email
- Rushing to get to the post office before it closes
- Organizing files and folders
- Tidying your desk
- Booking a dentist appointment

For these tasks, you may find that you perform faster and with more accuracy if you slightly up the pressure:

- Play some upbeat music
- Set the timer to countdown to a deadline
- Stack the task with another low-stakes task
- Challenge yourself to do a little more

Not only will you get these tasks done quicker and more efficiently, but you'll probably also enjoy them more.

Have you ever had a day where it felt like you were racing around like a headless chicken, and yet instead of feeling depleted, you almost got a buzz out of it? Chances are you were nicely within the optimal zone.

By the same token, if you've ever had a day where you had barely anything to do and yet those few activities felt like a tedious chore you had to drag your feet through, then it may have been that you were suffering too little physiological arousal!

Use Mild Stress as a Motivator—But Don't Manufacture It

Can a strategic stress increase sharpen focus and boost performance? Absolutely.

But that stress needs to be:

- Discrete
- Short term
- Intentional

Manufacturing chronic, vague, unnecessary, and artificial stressors is just asking for trouble.

Don't force urgency.

Some people who "thrive under pressure" have gotten into the habit of deliberate procrastination in order to harness that pre-deadline panic. Others leave things to the last minute and then cram.

But this is not sustainable. Adrenaline is a poor substitute for focus, and panic may get the thing done, but at what cost?

Instead, when it comes to stress management, think in terms of sustainability:

- Consider joining accountability groups that will encourage you to meet deadlines in good time.
- Build in plenty of short-term rewards along the way.
- Work in brief but ultra-focused "sprints"—your arousal level will be high, but you take a break before you tip over into chronic stress.

Summary

- Because gaming relies on the skills of observation, filtering for relevance, and taking strategic action, it can be a platform for cultivating better focus, working memory, problem-solving, critical thinking, attention control, and adaptability. **The right game can count as "flow practice" with transferable benefits.**
- **Games can be mental gyms** helping you to practice the skills you wish to acquire, whether that's better focus, impulse control or improved working memory.
- Working memory is limited. **Deep learning requires effective cognitive load management.** Self-regulate by reducing cognitive load where possible—manage intrinsic load, reduce extraneous load, and strategically leverage germane load (i.e. schemas, mental frameworks, analogies, or visual aids).
- Experiment with chunking, simplify and condense material, use story and visual aids, and continually find ways to eliminate distractions, noise, and clutter. Increase germane load by linking new knowledge to existing knowledge networks.
- Use the Yerkes-Dodson curve to **proactively manage stress** and arousal

levels, so you learn optimally. **A moderate level of stress can enhance performance, focus, creativity, and retention,** while too little or too much can hinder it. With **self-awareness + metacognition** you can maintain optimal arousal levels.
- Match the task difficulty with your stress level (complex tasks usually need lower arousal levels) and make use of mild, limited stress to motivate yourself.

Chapter 4: Learning is a Dialogue

How Asking the Right Questions Fuels Deep Learning

"To ask the right question is already half the solution of a problem."

- **Carl Jung**

Shallow learning is simply about *acquisition*—we encounter a new fact or idea that we don't currently possess, we add it to our pile, and now it's ours.

But deep learning is about *comprehension*—we approach an unknown phenomenon, we engage with it, and then an almost magical transformation happens—we understand.

One of the crucial differences between deep and shallow learning is the quality of our engagement with the unknown. There is a special name for the right attitude to take the unknown: **curiosity**.

And one of the purest expressions of curiosity is of course a question.

Every instance of true learning starts with a question. Even the scientific method itself—i.e. one of mankind's surest paths to knowledge—is really just a formalized version of question asking.

But not all questions are the same!

Some are superficial. Others are expansive, prompting greater reflection and illumination.

Some are big, others small.

Some questions open up the possibility of genuine learning, others make learning impossible.

You may have heard "there's no such thing as a stupid question," but there sure is such a thing as an *irrelevant* question, or one that brings you no closer to real learning.

The quality of your questions determine the quality of the answers you get... which determines the quality of your learning.

Here are some practical ways to ask higher quality questions.

Connect Tools to Real-World Problems

Let's say you're trying to learn something new, like a programming language.

As you make your way around the new concepts, you might find yourself asking questions of a certain order:

- "What is this?"
- "Why does it work like that?"
- "How do I work through this exercise?"
- "How does this chapter fit with the other stuff I've just learned?"

These questions are great and will help you lay a good foundation.

But we can kick things up a notch by asking questions of a higher order:

- "Where could I actually apply this idea?"
- "How would this tool solve the real problems I'm facing in life right now?"
- "How can I make this concept or tool actionable?"
- "Why does any of this actually matter in the world? Or to me?"

We can go even further, and make our questions metacognitive by asking questions about our own question-asking process:

- "What kind of answers am I getting to these questions? Are they useful? Could I ask different ones?"
- "This new tool I'm learning about is like an answer to a question. What question is

> it answering? What problems is it solving?"
> - "How would I have to think about this idea in order to apply it elsewhere? What might I not be seeing here?"

Deep learning is flexible and can **shift from abstract/theoretical to practical—and back again.**

If something is abstract, ask how it can be applied, why, and when.

If something is practical, ask questions that will reveal the broader underlying principles.

Either way, be aware that questions always vary in quality, and can shed light on different levels of comprehension—either at the level of the task itself **(intra-task),** or concerning the application of that task relative to its context, your goals and values, and to other tasks **(inter-task).**

Understand this and you empower yourself to use questions mindfully and proactively.

Use Probing Questions to Deepen Understanding

It may be more accurate to talk about a *string* of questions leading to comprehension, rather than just a one-and-done question that reveals all.

Follow-up questions are a way to **dialogue** with the unknown.

Ask a question.

Listen carefully to the answer.

Take this answer and ask another related question.

It's the **back-and-forth** that gradually shows us our own blind spots and knowledge gaps and allows us to refine our comprehension and correct misunderstandings.

- If you've asked yourself a question and answered it, don't stop there. Ask, "Can I explain how I got that answer?"
- If you're asking questions about a process, and you're beginning to understand it, ask yourself, "Can I think of an example of this in action?"
- If you're learning about a law or general principle, ask yourself, "Is this always true, though? When is this not the case?" Then you can follow up *that* question with another: "What does this exception tell me about the rule?"
- If you're learning about a range of new ideas and concepts, ask yourself which is most important and fundamental. Once you've found the answer, don't stop there.

Ask a follow up: "*Why* is this the most important or fundamental?"

You get the idea. **Questions are tools**, and they need to change and adapt as your understanding grows.

Consider an example: You're briefly learning about the concept of supply and demand in economics.

Question: What is this?

Answer: Supply is the ability of a market to produce goods or services, and demand is the ability of that market to desire those goods or services. The relationship between availability and desire determines price.

Follow up question: So what happens when supply exactly meets demand?

Follow up answer: You reach equilibrium, which is the stable "market clearing price."

Follow up question: Wait, is that always true? Are there any products that *don't* behave this way?

Follow up answer: Yes. One example is so-called *Veblen Goods*: luxury goods where the high price itself is part of the desirability. Here, increased price = increased demand.

Follow up question: Interesting. So how could this idea solve the real problems I'm facing in life right now?

Follow up answer: You're trying to market your products as luxurious, right? You might want to consider increasing your prices, not decreasing them.

Follow up question: Hmm, sounds a little unethical. What about conspicuous *under*consumption? Might there be a way to charge people more for something that they believe will indirectly lead to less consumption over time?

Follow up answer: Well, there's this other economic concept called…

You get the idea. This *strategic string* of questioning takes you far off the pages of your economics textbook and is likely to result in a richer, more three-dimensional understanding of the concepts at hand.

Importantly, through this process you are the one asking questions… *and you are the one answering them!*

Self-questioning is a way to pattern your own structured, deliberate exploratory process.

Create a Culture of Collaborative Inquiry

You don't have to literally have that little question mark to create an atmosphere of curiosity, receptiveness, and genuine inquiry.

Ask good questions *with others*. Invite them into your deep learning process.

When you create an atmosphere of genuine inquiry, you turn other people into collaborators and co-explorers.

There is an art to asking other people the right questions.

"What do you think?" = Pretty generic feedback. Cliché, boring.

What questions are likely to yield more value?

- "What am I/are we missing here?"
- "Here's my idea… what do you think, can you spot any problems?"
- "What's your perspective on XYZ? This is how it seems to me…"
- "I'm stumped. Why do *you* think this didn't work?"
- "What assumptions are we making?"

If we're defensive, egotistical, or overly competitive, it's easy to see other people as threats or adversaries. But other people—and their unique views on things—can often be the secret ingredient that helps our own understanding click into place.

Proactively set up generative and constructive dialogues with team members. Pose questions not just of yourself but of them, and of the process.

- When studying some new theory or idea: "What are the core assumptions of this model? What type of model is it?"
- When putting together a business plan: "In what type of market would this approach fail? Where do you think it would succeed?"
- When trying to grasp a physiological/medical process: "What happens when this mechanism breaks down?"
- When working on personal development: "Can you see a blind spot I'm not seeing? What core beliefs might a person who is doing what I'm doing have?"

Of course, we want to make sure that we aren't just asking philosophical questions for the sake of it, or to appear intelligent or engaged. **Our questions need to be meaningfully connected to the current stage of our inquiry.**

What are you trying to do—Explore consequences? Brainstorm alternatives? Uncover cause and effect relationships?

Tailor your questions accordingly.

Ultimately: **"Is this question going to help me take an important next step?"**

Or to put it another way: **"What question should I ask in order to take that important next step?"**

Good questions don't just passively fill knowledge gaps. They activate curiosity, and set in motion real, interactive processes of insight.

Pre-Testing and Quizzing Yourself: A Shortcut to Deep Learning

"The greatest enemy of knowledge is not ignorance, it is the illusion of knowledge."
- **Stephen Hawking**

One way to ask yourself important and revealing questions is to quiz yourself.

Though self-quizzing may seem fairly simple and obvious, the "testing effect" as it's called in cognitive science is a powerful way of turning passive study into an active deep learning process.

Have you ever studied for ages for an exam, only to sit down on the day and find that your mind has gone completely blank?

It's incredibly frustrating—at the time you studied, you truly felt like you understood all the material, and felt confident in what you knew.

So what happened?

The answer is that you failed to train recall.

In fact, certain study approaches can mean that exam day is actually the *first time* you're asking your brain to recall that information. The blankness you feel? That's actually your true level of understanding—and your prior perception of confidence was an illusion.

- Reviewing
- Reading
- Re-reading
- Highlighting
- "Going over" notes

We've already seen that these kinds of activities keep you busy and make you *feel* like you're doing something—but what are you really doing?

The thing that truly counts is recall because (in an exam situation at least) recall is the only way to outwardly demonstrate your retention.

If you cannot retrieve everything you've mentally embedded, then you haven't learned.

It's not enough to be familiar with the content.

It's not enough to recognize it.

It's not enough to run your eyes over the words and, for that brief moment, "understand" it.

The thing that truly shows whether you've truly grasped a concept is if you can recall it from memory and reproduce it. This is why testing is so important: *because it constantly reveals your actual level of mastery.*

That means you have a precious opportunity to zoom in on weak spots and fix them now... instead of waiting until exam day to discover that your grasp is weaker than you thought.

- Reading and re-reading? That only trains your reading muscles.
- Practicing recall? That trains your recall muscles.

Pre-testing means sitting down and breezing through your exam paper, because by that point, it's something you've already done dozens of times before.

Passing or failing a practice test? That's not what's important.

The value of self-testing lies in what it shows us about our own learning process. After all, much of what we learn never undergoes the corrective process of formal testing. That means that the things in life we are never tested on? Those are the things where the "illusion of knowledge" poses the greatest risk.

Don't assume, test.

Every time you retrieve a fact, solve a problem, or explain a concept without consulting your notes, you're cultivating a more durable, more connected sense of understanding.

Start with Pre-Testing—Even Before You "Know" the Material

Reading and re-reading notes may feel comforting, and it's certainly a task you can do with half a brain at times! Unfortunately, spending hours this way brings you little gain—even if you're going to the effort of diligently marking your notes up with colored highlighters.

Self-test, and do it often.

Plan mini quizzes all along your study journey:

- **Before** you even start, to prime your brain and get it alert and on the lookout for relevant material when it encounters it.

- **During** the process of learning, to guide and shape your engagement.
- **After** you've learned some new information, to check your retention.

You do not need to wait till you understand everything to test yourself—testing yourself is *how* you begin to understand everything!

Use a few short questions, snippets from an actual exam paper, or practice questions, even if they're of your own making.

Tip: You can also jot down a few questions you have about the upcoming information. This way, as you work through it, your brain will be actively looking for answers, meaning you engage more deeply.

Your brain always wants to reduce uncertainty, so if you pose a question but don't answer it, you boost engagement as your brain actively seeks to close that open loop.

Pre-testing:

- Boosts your curiosity and engagement.
- Shows you what you already know and understand.
- Encourages you to actively consider what you are expected to learn from the upcoming material.

Before reading a chapter or watching a lecture, write down 3 – 5 questions you think might be answered. Even if you get them wrong, you're training your brain to anticipate and retain what's coming. Later, answer the same questions again to measure your progress.

Another great side effect of pre-testing is that it gives you something to compare your progress against.

Use Self-Quizzing to Pinpoint Gaps and Direct Focus

It is so, so, so tempting as a student to simply focus on what you *already* know.

It feels familiar and safe, and you get the irresistible confirmation that comes with the thought, "Yup, I really get this. I understand this. I know my work."

Two things:

1. What benefit is there in revising what you already know?
2. Are you sure you *really* know it? Or are you just really used to reading it?

Self-testing is a lot less fun because you don't get that instant, satisfying hit of recognition... but you get something better!

Self-testing forces you to look at what you *don't* know, and devise a roadmap for getting better.

Self-testing doesn't have to be prolonged or complicated to be effective:

- Read a paragraph or a page, close the book and then recite out loud from memory everything you've learned. Then open the book, and see what you missed. Highlight *that*. Later, try again, this time focusing on those highlighted pieces.
- Break a practice test paper down into chunks and complete a few questions after the relevant section in your material.
- Devise your own questions—for example, you can convert section headings or titles into questions, collect a few, and periodically pause to quiz yourself (example, "The beginning of the Roman Empire" becomes "What year did the Roman Empire officially begin?").
- Challenge yourself to reproduce charts, diagrams, and flowcharts as you encounter them.

Simulate Real Test Conditions to Build Confidence and Recall

"Test conditions" for you may not entail sitting down to a literal written test.

Test conditions might be:

- A musical recital or other performance
- A meeting or presentation
- An important interview
- A sports game or athletic performance
- A complicated surgery or procedure
- A challenging event

Of course, some of us do go blank during exams or forget everything we've learned not because we haven't done enough self-testing, but because our self-testing hasn't been a true instance of active recall.

The speech you practiced delivering in the comfort of your own home to your cat on the sofa suddenly seems to stick in your throat when you're in a giant room packed with dozens of people, bright lights blinding you.

Real life conditions contain:

- Heightened stress and anxiety
- Increased levels of extraneous cognitive load
- Increased unpredictability—they're not as much in our control

To gain more lasting confidence in our practice sessions, our self-testing needs to reflect real test conditions as closely as possible.

- Do a few dry runs of your performance in the venue you'll actually be using.

- Tackle the task at the same time of day, wearing the same clothes, with the same annoyances and impediments that might meet you on the day.
- Use accurate time limits. If time pressure is required of the for-real performance, make it a feature of your practice and testing.
- Make sure you're doing a complete run-through, no stops, no breaks, no checking of notes.

Honestly? Doing a true-to-life run like this is not much fun and can be cognitively demanding. But in the long run, you'll actually feel **more confident** and **less anxious**—because when you get up on that stage, or sit in that hot seat, it won't be your first time.

Prediction Before Instruction: Spark Curiosity to Boost Retention

"If knowledge is power, then curiosity is the muscle."

- **Danielle LaPorte**

So, where do we go from here?

We know that pre-testing boosts curiosity and engagement, priming your brain to actively seek out relevant information, and retain that information better when it discovers it.

In this section, we'll dig a little deeper into this concept and discover that our conventional ideas around testing may be backwards—i.e., that "testing" may be more useful before we encounter new material than after.

Learning isn't just a cognitive phenomenon; it's an emotional one. You are not just a neutral machine, waiting to be passively programmed with new information or skills.

- You learn on some level because you *want* to learn.
- You ask questions because you're genuinely *curious* about the answer.
- You seek mastery with a new skill because you *desire* that mastery.

Curiosity, wanting, desire... these are the emotional aspects that give learning its real purpose and direction.

Without these things, you're just consuming.

Enter the concept called "**prediction before instruction**" (Brod, 2021, *Predicting as a learning strategy*; Brod et. al., 2018).

It's simple; before instruction (i.e. before encountering new information, a lesson, training prompts, teaching, or coaching of any kind), spend a little time making a few predictions.

How accurate these predictions are doesn't matter in the least.

What matters is that you're activating an internal sense of curiosity which prepares your brain for deeper and more meaningful retention of new information. It goes like this:

1. You make a prediction about the upcoming material
2. You now feel ever so slightly curious
3. This curiosity triggers a small dopamine release
4. This dopamine plays a key role in increasing your motivation and attention
5. The answer/resolution arrives, and it really "clicks"
6. More dopamine is released, creating a feeling of reward
7. This feeling makes the new information much more memorable

Curiosity opens up a little gap—the desire to close that gap provides an important impetus to engage deeply and actively seek out answers.

Curiosity is a tool.

Are you struggling with low motivation? Your real struggle may be with low curiosity. "If I know what I shall find, I do not want to find it."

But if you *don't* know what lies ahead? Then your curiosity becomes an engine that drives you towards it. You're suddenly more motivated.

Deliberately cultivating pre-task curiosity is not some new-fangled learning technique. Rather, it's exactly why the brain's inbuilt reward system exists in the first place!

The dopamine system is incredibly complex, but the brain has evolved certain finely tuned processes involving anticipation, pleasure, and fulfilment in order to shape and direct the learning process.

Real curiosity about what we're learning is not a nice side effect—it's a crucial ingredient.

Today, sadly, many of us have rather convoluted reasons for pursuing our various goals, and any natural and spontaneous curiosity we may have once had for our subject has long since given way to routine.

Employing curiosity before you dive into material re-engages this natural curiosity, and helps us re-discover that learning is an innately rewarding experience.

When you ask

- "What happens next?"
- "Where is this line of reasoning going?"
- "Can I see any problems on the horizon?"

...then you are no longer a passive consumer of information, but an active investigator in a deliberate learning process.

Making predictions = asking questions = formulating hypotheses.

Whenever you do this, you're more alert, more hopeful, more motivated, and more proactive. You are primed for deep learning. Whether you find the answers to your questions or not, your process is already more rewarding than it might have been!

Let's take a closer look at practical ways to incorporate "prediction before instruction."

Start with a Curiosity Question

Make a promise to yourself that you will never just sit down to a task or a new piece of information and just mindlessly take it in.

Before anything new—whether that's a video, a journal article, an exercise, or a tutorial—pause and ask yourself a question.

What kind of question?

That's easy: a question you're *genuinely* curious to know the answer to!

That may be:

- "Who wrote this news article and why?"
- "How much about this topic do I already know?"
- "Wait, what is a hippocampus?"

By posing a question, you put yourself into immediate dialogue with the material. You will now pay close attention to determine whether your prediction is confirmed or refuted. It's this close attention that deepens your learning.

Try marking up papers or textbooks with your questions. You could even scribble a question in the margins. Now, when you review, you can more closely follow your own evolving path of understanding, and the material will take on a more engaging question-and-answer format

Important: The question itself doesn't matter. The curiosity does.

For this method to work, you need to *genuinely* feel a spark of interest. If you really don't care about the answer to a question, don't bother asking it. Avoid making up a performative question just because it seems like the kind of thing you should want to know. If you can't think of a good question, that's OK, move on. But at least give your brain the *opportunity* to form a genuine, original response to the material.

Make a Quick Guess Before You Begin

Remember the growth mindset we discussed in chapter 1?

Most schools, universities and workplaces *do not* operate from this mindset. Their passive default is that mistakes are unfortunate, unwanted, and embarrassing, and that getting something wrong is a sign that you haven't learned something properly (whereas the truth is that getting things wrong is *how* you learn properly).

Making guesses is valuable, *even if your guesses are wrong.*

There is value in active engagement, period. When we pause and invite ourselves to anticipate what's coming, we're firing up our reward system and recruiting our brain's inbuilt power to learn.

Again, the accuracy of your guess doesn't matter—what matters is the frame of mind the guess triggers. You are not just passively taking something in, but now have "skin in the game." You are present and taking part.

- Before watching a video tutorial: "How do I think they're going to approach this problem?"

- Before reading a journal article: "Can I guess their research methodology?"
- Before skimming a news article "What exactly do I think happened here?"

Important: You are not blindly entertaining assumptions and biases; in fact, your job is to pay close attention when a guess is *wrong*. Where did your guess come from? What does this tell you?

The correction and adjustment you make in the light of new information will be more meaningful to you than if you had simply encountered that information without making a prediction first.

Reflect on What Surprised You

Similarly, get into the habit of asking yourself afterwards:

- "Is that what I expected?"
- "What was I surprised by?"
- "What have I learned that I was not expecting to learn?"

Again, remember that this questioning technique is not primarily about the content of what you're learning, but about the learning process itself.

You are not merely giving yourself a test like the ones you received at school, in order to see whether you've passed or failed. It's not about ranking or appraising the value of your output.

Instead, you are simply curious about *how* you are learning.

There's no need to pounce on things you've overlooked or misunderstood and frame them as mistakes or blind spots. Instead, *frame them as pleasant surprises.*

Instead of triggering shame and regret, allow awareness of these things to create a feeling of interest and wonder in you.

Reflecting in this way makes learning:

- More fun
- More personal
- More memorable
- Less threatening/stressful

Use the PACE Framework

In an interesting 2019 paper titled *How Curiosity Enhances Hippocampus-Dependent Memory: The Prediction, Appraisal, Curiosity, and Exploration (PACE) Framework*, researchers Gruber and Ranganath propose a model that puts curiosity at the center of learning.

PACE stands for Prediction → Appraisal → Curiosity → Exploration

The idea here is that curiosity is actually a result of *prediction errors.*

Step 1: You make a prediction.

Step 2: You go out and gather information to confirm or deny the prediction, and discover errors, unexpected content, or gaps.

Step 3: Depending on how your brain processes these errors, the result is either curiosity or anxiety/fear.

Step 4: If curiosity, the response is to explore (that is, learn!). If anxiety, the response is to defend and retreat.

Not surprisingly, the authors feel that it is when we are in *exploration* mode that we experience better memory, better attention, and overall better learning. Importantly, the process above is cyclical, meaning that curiosity can trigger exploration that then creates further predictions, so the cycle repeats.

One big takeaway? The mind that is curious, open, receptive, and exploratory is the mind that is capable of deep learning.

Pay close attention to feelings of anxiety, dread, or fear. If you notice your joy and curiosity have dampened, pause and get back into exploratory mode by making a prediction, finding a way to appraise it, and slowly build real curiosity again.

Clarifying Concepts by Teaching Yourself

"I don't know what's the matter with people: they don't learn by understanding, they learn by some other way—by rote or something. Their knowledge is so fragile!"

- **Richard Feynman**

There's a long-standing cultural connection between "talking to yourself" and having a screw loose.

The truth is that "self-explanation" may actually be a mark of intelligence, and one of the most underutilized ways to access deep learning.

Having reached this point in the book, you can probably already guess why "teaching yourself" may be a good idea:

- It's active, not passive, which means. you construct knowledge, not just consume it.
- It helps you connect what you don't yet know to what you do; i.e., create scaffolding and occupy the ZPD/flow zone.

- It increases your curiosity and engagement.
- It encourages you to think independently, not resorting to mere repetition or habit.
- It forces you, in a sense, to "test" your comprehension, rather than just assume it.

Self-explanation encourages you to **reflect, reason, and integrate**. People who are fast learners are often really good at this without knowing it—it is as though they have their own internalized "mini teacher" who is constantly walking them through the learning process.

Talk Yourself Through Worked Examples

When a team of cognitive psychologists and education experts reviewed over 700 research studies on 10 common learning techniques, they were able to identify those methods that produced genuine results... and those that really didn't.

They explain:

> "Cognitive and educational psychologists have developed and evaluated numerous techniques, ranging from re-reading to summarizing to self-testing, for more than 100 years. Some common strategies

markedly improve student achievement, whereas others are time-consuming and ineffective. Yet this information is not making its way into the classroom. Teachers today are not being told which learning techniques are supported by experimental evidence, and students are not being taught how to use the ones that work well. In fact, the two study aids that students rely on the most are not effective. One of them may even undermine success."

"Psychologists Identify the Best Ways to Study" Dunlosky et. al., 2013, *Scientific American*.

The researchers wanted to identify the study techniques that reliably produced results in a wide range of situations and topics. So what did they find?

The winners:

1. Self-testing
2. Distributed practice (or spaced repetition)
3. Elaborative interrogation (or, asking questions)
4. Self-explanation
5. Interleaved practice

What *didn't* stand out as useful was, ionically, the default in most learning institutions today:

reading and re-reading, highlighting, taking notes, watching videos, and rote memorization.

Let's look at number 4: self-explanation. You may recognize this as another version of Vygotsky's "self-instruction."

Mental training wheels are always verbal. When we carefully talk ourselves through a process, we are teaching our brain to make those pathways permanent so that in time they become automatic and we no longer need the explanation at all.

When you were little, you probably did this when learning to tie your shoelace:

> "OK, first I have to take this piece, and make a loop… good… OK wait hold that a little more tightly, then I need to pick up the other piece and wrap it around… like that… still keep a hold of the previous piece… then next I have to…"

Today, you tie your shoelaces completely on autopilot, but it's only because your original self-instruction was so deliberate.

It's the same when we learn anything.

Whenever you're working through examples or exercises, slow down. Walk yourself through them step by step.

Ask yourself questions and find your way to the answers.

- "Hm, are you stuck? What do you need to do next?"
- "Now, what is the concept that you're using here?"
- "I'm going to use this tool. But why not the other tool? *This* one is more appropriate because..."
- "Do you remember why this step matters? Yes, it's so that we avoid mistakes with units later on."

One group of researchers found that asking these kinds of questions measurably increased the comprehension of test participants as they solved chemistry problems (Pease et. al., 2013).

You can also include encouragement and acknowledgement of progress. Remember, **curiosity and a sense of reward are important parts of the learning process:**

- "Good. You've done that right."
- "Yes, this makes sense, let's keep exploring this idea."
- "That worked really well. My prediction was correct."
- "Keep going!"

For example, if you're learning how to balance chemical equations, say: "OK so I'm adding this coefficient here and here, to make sure both sides have the same number of oxygen atoms. Why? Because that's the law of conservation of mass, and it's an equation, so the sides must be equivalent. Good job for remembering that."

It may feel silly to speak out loud this way, but it's *really* helpful!

Don't just work mentally through the steps. Speak out loud to yourself. Be a teacher. Don't assume that the steps are so easy and obvious that you already know them—speaking them out loud will reveal to you whether you do or not.

Use Self-Explanation When Reading

Your learning may not require worked examples or things like math or chemistry problems. Fortunately, self-explanation can be applied to study of *all* kinds, including reading.

Now, it's worth understanding the difference between self-testing, asking questions and self-explanation.

When we self-explain, we are doing just that— **generating explanations** for the phenomena we encounter.

An explanation is not just a regurgitation of information. It's a narrative, a reason, a justification or an account that helps *make sense* of something, often making cause-and-effect or logic statements.

The physicist Richard Feynman understood that on a very deep level, most of us possess only fake understanding, because our explanations are superficial, illusory, or circular. In other words, they don't explain anything. They merely describe.

Let's return to that previous example: Why do there need to be equal numbers of oxygen atoms on either side of the chemical equation?

- Because that's what I did last time, and it worked
- Because that's what the tutor said to do
- Because of the equals sign—both sides must be equal
- Because of the conservation of mass

Only one of the above is a real *explanation*.

Similarly, consider how your comprehension might change if you were reading about, say, the American civil war. How might you *explain* the start of this war?

- It started because of slavery
- It started because the north wanted to halt the south's expansion of slavery into new territories
- It was triggered by economic differences between the north and south, and

disagreements about the reach of the Federal government

If I answer "slavery" to the above question, have I actually provided an explanation? Sort of. But no more than when I say that the oxygen atoms on either side of a chemical equation have to be equal because it's an equation, and that's what equations are like...

Some explanations are not explanations, but superficial descriptions. They reveal that we don't really *understand* the phenomena at hand.

Without taking the time to work through your own self-explanation, you may content yourself with "The civil war was fought because of slavery," without considering what that actually means.

Granted, the American civil war is complex and there probably isn't a single easy "explanation"—but by forcing yourself to find one, you are giving yourself the chance to come to that conclusion yourself.

If you keep asking yourself, **"How do I know this?"** you open doors to deeper comprehension that goes beyond rote or superficial descriptions.

Teach It Back, Even If Just to Yourself

The idea is simple: **If you can't comfortably explain something to a five-year-old, then you don't really understand that concept yourself.**

For various perplexing psychological reasons, it's often easier to *feel* like you comprehend something than it is to actually comprehend it.

Remove jargon and all those ready-made, second-hand explanations and you will soon see if you truly grasp the concept underneath.

If you teach yourself, or imagine yourself explaining the concept as though to a layperson or child, your blind spots and assumptions will quickly become apparent.

Consider: You might "know" what electricity is. You might have learned by heart a kind of standard definition: "Electricity is the flow of electrical charge," and you might know that it has something to do with electrons and how they move.

But pause for a moment.

What, then, is electrical charge?

To say that electricity is about electrical charge is a little like saying a circular definition is a definition that is circular.

If you were forced to *explain* electricity to someone who also didn't understand the terms "electrical charge" or "atoms", how might you go about it?

The ease with which you can do this reveals your real understanding!

It's not enough to have excellent memory and diligently recall all the right *words* to describe a certain phenomenon. True understanding comes from deeply understanding what those words mean.

- **Try the "Explain Like I'm Five" Test** – pPractice explaining the idea to a child or layperson unfamiliar with the topic. Notice where you get stuck and why. The child or layperson can be imaginary, but real is best!
- **Teach your peers** – Take turns explaining concepts to a study partner and solicit their questions and feedback.
- **Imagine teaching past-you** – Picture a version of yourself a few levels back and address this person as you concoct an explanation that would help them make sense of your current material.

Summary

- Deep learning is characterized by an attitude of **genuine curiosity**, which is expressed in the form of a question. **The**

quality of your question determines the quality of your learning process.
- **Self-questioning is a way to pattern your own deliberate learning process.** Ask questions that connect material to real world problems, or help you shift from abstract/theoretical to practical, and back again. Ask probing, meaningful follow-up questions to establish a kind of collaborative dialogue with the unknown.
- **Pre-testing and self-quizzing** activates deeper learning. Testing reveals your true retention and provides opportunities for improvement—focus on what you *don't* yet know. Quiz yourself before, during, and after new material, and simulate real test conditions to practice.
- **Prediction before instruction** sparks curiosity, boosts motivation, and invites to proactively engage with material. Start with a question, make quick guesses and then reflect on what surprises you. The PACE framework (Prediction → Appraisal → Curiosity → Exploration) harnesses curiosity to drive deep learning. Remember that **making guesses is valuable, even if your guesses are wrong. Embrace prediction errors.**

- **Clarify concepts by teaching yourself.** Self-explanation encourages you to **reflect, reason, and integrate**. Explain concepts as though to a child to identify knowledge gaps. Maintain a teacher-student dialogue, even if just with yourself.

Chapter 5: The Many Languages of Learning

Vocabulary Instruction and Deep Learning: Unlocking the Power of Words

"The limits of my language mean the limits of my world."

- **Ludwig Wittgenstein**

Words are symbols. We use them to point to concepts, but they are *not* the concepts themselves.

This is a pretty basic observation, right? Yet often we fail to learn as deeply as we could precisely because we forget the difference and assume that if we possess certain words and the ability to manipulate them, then in some way we also possess the concept.

Used well, words can help us illuminate a path to knowledge and understanding.

Used poorly, words can get in the way.

An impressive vocabulary has always been associated with intelligence, but why? Research has found that high-vocabulary individuals not only know more words, but actually have a richer understanding of their meaning (Curtis et al., 1987, Cronbach 1942). Repeatedly it's found that people have the best grasp of a word when their understanding is:

- **Generalized** – They understand the definition and the deeper meaning.
- **Decontextualized** – They understand that meaning in an abstract sense, and can see how to use it in a wide variety of situations.
- **Precise** – They grasp correct and incorrect uses of the word, and can discern its meaning compared to other closely related words.
- **Available** – They're able to call on the word in thinking or in real world communication.

As you can see, it's not mere possession of a word and its associated definition that counts. What matters is *how that word is used*—**the most masterful learners tend to be those who understand that words are tools.**

Consider for example the word "monitor."

Do you know the definition of this word? And how to use it? Do you *really* know the phenomenon this symbol is pointing to?

Moderate language users may give a limited, context-dependent definition:

- "It means to watch someone."
- "It's basically a computer screen."
- "It's a person at school they put in charge of something, like a hall monitor."

Advanced language users, on the other hand, will be able to grasp the deeper meaning (not just the definition) of the word, which comes from the Latin for *one that warns* or *overseer*. Because of their deeper understanding, they can clearly see the link between all three superficial definitions above, as well as imagine all sorts of new applications.

Even if, for example, they one day encounter the term *monitor* being used to describe a type of historical warship, they can instantly understand the meaning being conveyed. This understanding comes from their grasp of the *deeper generalized meaning* of the vocabulary, and not just adequate memorization of a specific definition.

Truly understanding a word involves more than just recognizing its definition; it means knowing how to use that word, how it connects to other words, and how exactly it fits into the world.

Even if your learning doesn't directly involve reading, writing, or language, it almost certainly is conveyed to you at least somewhat through the medium of words.

- Shallow, ineffective vocabulary acquisition = using language in limited, repetitive, and imprecise ways = passive, superficial learning.
- Deep, intentional vocabulary acquisition = using words in rich, meaningful, and strategic ways = effective, lasting and transformative learning.

A "rich" vocabulary, therefore, isn't the same as a large or exotic one. Being familiar with lots of different words doesn't make you an intelligent or insightful thinker any more than owning a house full of expensive instruments makes you a musician.

It used to be common to challenge yourself to learn a new vocabulary word every day in the hopes that this would make you a more sophisticated language user. What normally happens? You think, "Huh, *obsequious*. Cool word" and then promptly forget about it for the rest of your life.

If you want to acquire *deep* language proficiency, below are some proven approaches.

Use Words in Meaningful Contexts, Not Just Definitions

Avoid: Dry, abstract dictionary definitions.

Instead go for: Real world, everyday, relatable explanations, especially if you generate them yourself.

Step 1: When you encounter a useful new word, get acquainted. Learn the accurate definition (sometimes, understanding the etymology or the word's historical roots helps you get to the heart of its meaning) and then paraphrase this concept in your own words.

Step 2: Think of as many different contexts as possible where you could use this word. Werner and Kaplan's classic study showed that people tend to build into their definitions the specific context in which they first encountered it (Werner and Kaplan, 1952). This can be limiting, however.

Counter the effect by deliberately seeing how flexible you can be in applying this word to other contexts. It may feel a bit old school, but experiment with literally jotting down a few "example sentences" to get the hang of what this word looks like in use.

Step 3: Now *use* the word, and use it in as many real-life contexts as possible. You want to

practice flexible application and generalizability.

Tools like hammers and spanners only come into their own when used to perform the function they were designed for. It's the same with words—you only really understand a word when you take it out for a spin and see what you can do with it!

Let's say you're learning to code and you've just encountered this word *array*.

You consult a lot of formal definitions but then paraphrase in your own words in a simplified way: "An array is a container that holds a collection of different values or variables."

Instead of just *memorizing* this definition, you *use* it. You keep your eyes peeled for other contexts where it may apply ("What a lovely array of cakes! You say they're all homemade?" and you keep encouraging yourself to use it in your coding studies.

You are not just "learning vocabulary."

You are learning *concepts*… and new vocabulary is the handle that lets you grasp those concepts.

Interact with Words Actively and Repeatedly

Words come alive according to how they're used. Comprehension and mastery are revealed when words are used as tools in flexible, deliberate ways.

The more often you use a word in various contexts, the more available that word becomes in all your future thinking and communication. You want to wire the new word in to your existing networks.

Memorization doesn't work.

What does work?

- Intentional repetition
- Reflection
- Strategic application
- Connection to existing knowledge

A definition is just static information, but a new word truly becomes your own when you start interacting with it. As soon as you encounter a new word, engage with it. Claim it and incorporate it into your world.

The more thoughtful and intentional you can be in the way you process a word's meaning, the more mastery you have over it.

- What are some synonyms and antonyms of this word?
- What are some closely related terms that are nevertheless different? In what precise way are they different? Can I

- think of an expression or situation that would distinguish between them?
- What are some examples of this word in use?
- Is this an everyday word or is it "domain specific"? A bit of both?
- How does this word connect to others I'm already familiar with?
- Are there any related idioms, expressions, analogues, or metaphors here? What do they teach me?
- Where is this word's natural "home", i.e., where is its use appropriate and where might it be inappropriate? Why?

For example:

You may encounter the word "insinuate" one day and realize you don't understand what it means. You check up on a definition and some synonyms (*suggest, hint, indicate*) and mull over the differences between them. You wonder why it's harder to find antonyms—what could be the *opposite* of "hint indirectly in an unpleasant way"? Could it be to blurt out directly? Or to hint in a pleasant way? Both?

You keep drawing links and find yourself clarifying the difference between *imply*, *infer*, and *insinuate*—all very different words. You practice using each in different situations in everyday life. You understand that "insinuate" has a rather legalistic feel, and is always delivered as though it were itself an insinuation.

When you learn that the word insinuate used to mean both "to introduce torturously", "to creep in", and "to enter (a document) on the official register" in the 16th century, your understanding of the undertones of this word deepens. You start to see that a person might slyly insinuate themselves into a situation, or that a sneaky clause might be insinuated into a contract.

One day you spot the word "sinuous" used to describe a river, and pause. Is there a connection? (Yes, there is!).

This is not just pedantry. By getting to know a vocabulary word on this level, **you are strengthening more than just your language prowess; you're teaching yourself to think.**

Develop "Word Consciousness" and Make Vocabulary Playful

Deep learners are curious, proactive, and adaptable.

And this is exactly how they use language—in curious, active, and adaptable ways.

Make language playful:

- Experiment with poetry, puns, and word play.
- Play word games that challenge you, whether it's scabble, crosswords, or more creative and open-ended activities.
- Look for metaphors and analogies wherever you can to strengthen mental scaffolding ("An array is a little like a printer's tray with lots of little boxes...").
- Read widely—serious and not so serious, academic and recreational, old and new, digital and print. Look for connections between *everything*.
- Keep a "new words" journal or even record certain snippets or favorite turns of phrase.

Multimodal Learning: How Images, Words and Movement Work Together to Spark Deep Understanding

"You think with your body, not with your brain."

- **Daniel Kahneman**

We've already seen that changing up the format of a task can reduce cognitive load and make concepts easier to understand.

In this chapter, we'll explore a related idea: Combining information from *two or more different learning channels* at the same time can improve understanding and recall.

In other words, **you learn better when you engage multiple parts of your brain simultaneously**. There are two related theories here:

1. **Dual Coding**—activating both the visual and verbal systems (Allan Paivio, 1971).
2. **Embodied Cognition**—strengthening the mind-body connection by pairing cognition with movement (Varela et. al., 1991; Wilson & Foglia, 2011; Ale et. al., 2022).

Both of the above combined create a kind of "multimodal" learning approach.

Research suggests that multimodal learning

- Reduces cognitive load
- Helps create more detailed memories
- Increases comprehension
- Encourages richer connections

The good news is that you probably already know more about Dual Coding than you realize and have already been deriving benefits from mixing modes.

The better news is that if you can *consciously* use this approach in your own deliberate learning practice, you stand to make even more meaningful, lasting gains.

So how exactly do we put dual encoding and embodied cognition to practice?

Draw It, Explain It, Speak it Out Loud

It's not difficult to make your learning sessions more multimodal—in fact, **the brain *loves* to learn in this way, since that's exactly what it evolved to do.**

Consider:

- Written language was invented around *3000 years ago.*
- Homo Sapiens has existed for around *300,000 years.*
- This means that written verbal expression has only been a part of the human experience *for a puny 1%* of the total time that modern human beings have existed!

For tens of thousands of years our most ancient ancestors learned what they needed to know not by sitting in artificial educational settings, but by *actively engaging* with the very environment in which they were trying to survive. On the other hand, the modern public education system we today call "school" was more or less invented in the 19th century.

Written language has certainly afforded us undeniable advantages, but we shouldn't forget that **rich, contextual, and embodied learning was our first mother tongue**. The words came much, much later!

Learning is best, most enjoyable, and *most natural* when it's a three dimensional, full-body, immersive experience.

How do you create this kind of learning experience? Here are some examples:

- Examine a chart or diagram while you listen to a spoken or recorded explanation of what it means.
- Practice converting written descriptions into diagram or infographic form, then converting them back again. When you revise, use both verbal and visual at the same time.
- Make liberal use of mind maps and other visual representation techniques to combine diagrams with words—develop your own symbols, color coding, icons, cartoons, maps, flowcharts, tables, timelines, sketches, and visual organization techniques to paint a vivid picture for your mind. Audibly talk yourself through the creation of these visual aids.

- Read out loud or follow along in a text as you listen to someone else read.
- Watch videos with the subtitles on—especially good for language learning, since you can hear the spoken word as you see how it's written.

Primarily, you're looking to send your brain the same message in two different ways simultaneously through two different channels—the ears and through the eyes.

You want to **link verbal and nonverbal processing** (remembering that it's often the nonverbal processing that is more ancient, and more readily accessible!).

Remember that you are not just adding pictures to words or vice versa. You're looking for ways to meaningfully represent concepts in different ways. **The power of Dual Coding comes from your brain's active attempts to integrate the two sources of information into a single integrated concept.** It's how it learns.

Use Multimedia, Then Embody the Idea

There is an undeniable link between movement and thought.

Have you ever noticed how children—the human beings most preoccupied with learning—never really keep still?

In her book *Activate: Deeper Learning through Movement, Talk, and Flexible Classrooms* author Katherine Mills Hernandez explains that the heart of deep learning is engagement, and that exercise primes the brain for learning, and helps it retain more of what it learns.

She even recommends that students spend the first few minutes of every class

- pacing the room and talking out loud
- doing jumping jacks
- or otherwise getting their bodies moving!

Physical activity fills the body with oxygen, boosts blood flow, improves waste removal, and tones our nervous system.

We all know that physical wellbeing and sufficient exercise is good for our mental health and for keeping our brains in good order. But the theory of Embodied Cognition goes much further than this.

Our brain is part of our body, and physical movement is good for our body.

But movement can also be a *way* to think.

The way our physical body interacts with its physical environment influences and shapes:

- The thoughts we think
- The feelings we feel
- The perspectives we take

Cognition, then, is not just a brain thing—purely internal, invisible, mental, and detached. Instead, it's dynamic.

If experience and understanding arise out of the interaction between our mind, body, and environment, then what does that imply? We can influence the way we think and learn by changing the way these three interact.

How?

Become more mindful and **use as much of your entire being as possible when you learn, revise, or solve problems:**

- As you watch a video, write down some notes, listen to a lecture or read an article, bring to the idea to life on your body—literally.
- Use hand gestures to physically represent ideas and concepts (for example, physically indicate in space the relative position of different organelles in a cell as you describe their function out loud).
- Act out certain movements as though you were rehearsing those movements for real (playing an instrument, cooking a meal, or following a route on a map).

- Match your body language and facial expression to what you're learning (add in emotional and contextual detail by changing your vocal delivery as you read a historical account—you'll remember certain historical speeches far better if you've heard them in your own voice!).
- Walk around as you listen to a recorded lecture or even walk yourself through a procedure (you may more easily recall bits of information if you connect them to different areas in your house).
- Make learning social where possible—the physical gestures, facial expressions, unique perspectives and languages of other people can be enriching and illuminating.

The goal is not to perform—in fact, you often *don't* want people to see you doing this! Don't worry if you feel a bit goofy. Your mission is simply dual coding, where one of the learning channels is your body. You want to *feel* the idea in action.

Pull It All Together—and Go for a Walk

One study (Ferrer & Laughlin, 2017) showed that when the physical activity of college students was increased, their academic performance invariably improved, too. After spending years learning online, the "Zoom fatigue" is real and teachers now encourage students of all ages to take frequent "brain breaks"—i.e., get up move!

- **Take a movement break.** Gor for a walk or jog to clear your head. Take a stretch break or simply change your posture and enjoy a few deep breaths.
- **Try walking *and* talking.** The combination is often illuminating. If you're stuck on a problem or trying to brainstorm, walk it out and think as you stroll, or go with a friend and chat through the idea with them while walking. This activates embodied cognition and can help things start to click into place.
- **Get physical**. Experiment with writing on a large whiteboard where you can really stretch out and practice big, swooping movements. Play with a cork board or get tactile with magnets. Stand instead of sitting.
- **Be multimodal**. Wherever possible, combine ears, eyes, and body all in one—and make it social, too. Move your body, speak out loud, and use audio and visual elements all in the same learning session.

If you've ever found yourself to be easily distractable, then multimodal methods may instinctively appeal to you—they're far less boring!

Your deep learning sessions can be as rich and multidimensional as your imagination can make them.

Example: For personal development, you've decided to learn more about how cars work, because you want the empowerment and freedom that comes with being able to repair your own vehicles.

To learn about engines specifically, you play around with making sketches of engines, showing all the main parts, and as you sketch you talk out loud to yourself, "These are pistons, this here is the crankshaft…"

Once in a while you pause, take a look at the diagram and actually mimic the various engine movements with your hands, cementing that mind-body link and helping you grasp the actual concept on a deeper, pre-verbal level.

You also make a written list of these components, and you hang this up in a garage near real physical specimens that you can pick up and feel. You watch videos of different engines in action.

You ask a friend if you can watch as they work on their car, asking them to talk you through their process. You love how different their explanation is to the ones you've seen on

YouTube and in textbooks! You make a few notes on your phone for some questions you'd like to research further when you get the time.

Later you're out walking with a different friend and ask him a few more questions about a specific kind of repair. That evening, when you get home, you close your eyes and visualize yourself "revising" the steps of the procedure he was talking about, trying to recall every detail, and literally moving your hands as you go...

This is rich, multimodal learning.

It's natural, it's intuitive, and it's extremely effective.

The Power of Perspective—Taking in Deep Learning

"It is a narrow mind which cannot look at a subject from various points of view."

- **George Eliot**

We live in a world today where "filter bubbles" and social media algorithms have siphoned people off into their own entirely separate universes, where they may become completely oblivious to opinions, beliefs, or ways of seeing that are not their own. "Main character syndrome" is rife, critical thinking is nearly extinct, and empathy is at an all-time low.

Conflict mediators and marriage counsellors already know that "perspective taking" (considering the experience of someone other than yourself) is necessary if we hope to understand one another and build lasting relationships.

But did you know that **perspective taking is also essential for true, deep learning**?

Perspective taking - Contemplating a situation, idea, or concept from a different viewpoint. This can be the viewpoint of someone else, but doesn't have to be. *Any time* we consider how things might look different depending on the way we're looking, we're playing in the realm of perspective.

The first step to being aware of and appreciating other perspectives is, ironically, being aware of your own, and understanding it *as a perspective*.

Open, flexible thinking is about so much more than getting along with other human beings. Collaboration, compassion, and better communication? Yes, they're absolutely a side-effect of "intellectual empathy." Being a "big picture" thinker, however, has many other benefits.

Being able to switch perspectives:

- Increases cognitive flexibility
- Boosts creativity and problem-solving
- Reduces implicit bias—which means fewer mistakes and faulty assumptions
- Cultivates true critical thinking
- Enhances resilience
- Improves decision-making
- Builds higher order reflection and deeper thinking
- Helps us to accurately see blind spots and improve upon flaws
- Allows us to be more responsive and persuasive leaders
- Creates an attitude of intellectual humility and curiosity

Being self-centered is not just unpleasant—it's unintelligent!

Perspective taking is not a "soft skill" that's nice to have, but a core learning strategy.

That's because when you can flexibly consider many different viewpoints, you are essentially expanding your world, taking in more data sources, and giving yourself the opportunity to craft a more sophisticated, more nuanced viewpoint yourself.

Whether or not your goals focus on empathy and compassion, here are some practical ways to start using the skill of perspective taking to improve your own deep learning practice.

Practice "Step In, Step Out, Step Back" to Challenge Assumptions

The bad news?

Human beings have a natural tendency towards egotism.

Our default is to place *ourselves*—and our perspective—at the center of things, sometimes to the extent that we forget that there are other possibilities at all.

Switching perspectives is cognitively demanding. It relies on:

- **Good working memory** – to hold all sorts of facts and details in mind.
- **Inhibitory control** – to shelve our own viewpoint while we actively entertain another.
- **Cognitive flexibility** – to reflect, ask questions, solve problems and manage a degree of ambiguity and the unknown.

If you struggle with perspective taking, don't beat yourself up—being self-centered is not necessarily a moral failing, but rather a cognitive shortcut! It's just *easier* to put our own experiences, assumptions, values, expectations, etc. at the center of the universe, and cast everyone else as a supporting character.

The trouble is that this results in a "narrow mind"—a kind of mind that is less creative, less resilient, less perceptive, and far less able to solve problems, learn, and evolve.

We need to actively choose to cultivate intellectual empathy. And that can be hard work!

Try this three-step technique to break out of any cognitive narrowness

Step 1: Step in – Step into someone else's world.

- "What do I think this person thinks, feels, believes, knows, expects, values, wants, or experiences?"
- "Why might they be thinking and feeling this way?"

Step 2: Step out – —Come back to your perspective, and consider what exactly has to change for you to better understand theirs.

- "What would I need, or what would I have to understand, in order to more fully grasp the above perspective?"
- "What gaps can I notice in my own perspective?"
- "What obstacles can I see getting in the way of me understanding this other perspective more fully?"
- "What more do I need to find out here?"

Step 3: Step back – —Take a step all the way out of the entire situation, and see both you and the other person. Switch from being an actor to an observer of actors. What do you notice?

- "When I zoom out, what I can see about the interaction of my perspective and theirs?"
- "How does my interpretation of the situation fit into the broader context? And theirs?"

There is a simpler variation of this approach. Imagine you are toggling through different "cameras" or viewpoints:

- How do you view things right now?
- How do you think *they* view things right now? Try on the viewpoint of every other person in the situation.
- How do they see you? What do they think you think?
- Zoom out and try to see the entire situation through neutral eyes. How might an uninvolved third party see things?

Broadly, this approach helps us identify areas of bias or blind spots that otherwise might skip our attention. It can be done with a person you're interacting with, or a fictional or imaginary person. You can even apply it to news articles and books, objects, artworks, or abstract ideas and concepts.

Here are some examples of how perspective switching might apply to deep learning:

- Use perspective switching to try to understand feedback or guidance you receive from tutors and teachers. What can they see that you can't? What might you need to really understand what they are trying to share with you?
- When you're stuck on something, find a peer who is not struggling and try to look into their technique, their attitude, and their overall approach to the problem. What makes them able to understand it when you can't?
- If you're trying to teach or explain a concept to someone else, do the process in reverse: Take their perspective to try and understand what they're not grasping, and why. Your own understanding may well improve!
- When in creative, innovative, or problem-solving mode, remind yourself that finding a solution is often just a question of changing the way you're looking at things. Literally imagine seeing through other people's eyes—how might *they* define or perceive this idea? Are there aspects that you are forgetting or overlooking?

Use the Four-Step Perspective-Taking Method to Resolve Conflicts

Learning Strategist Amy Lou Abernethy has a handy four-step perspective-taking method for effectively overcoming conflict.

Before you think, "I don't really need conflict-resolution strategies in my line of work," think again. **Conflict resolution is more or less misunderstanding management**—and for those of us interested in deep learning, we need every tool we can get to cut down on confusion and error!

The steps are:

1. Seek understanding
2. Ideate
3. Hypothesize
4. Observe and Adjust

We can follow the same four-step approach for both conflict resolution *and* deep learning:

- **Conflict resolution**
    - used externally
    - improves communication between different people
- **Deep learning**
    - used internally

- enhances your own comprehension and inner coherence

Let's take a closer look, with two examples:

Conflict resolution: You've just hired a new team member, who is acting like a know-it-all and failing to take direction from management. Their approach has meant they've now broken an expensive piece of equipment and are denying it.

Deep learning: You've been breezing through an algebra textbook but have suddenly hit a wall. A certain concept just does *not make sense* and you can't get around it. You're getting really frustrated.

Step 1: Seek understanding

It's natural to immediately start with our own goals and values, but choose instead to temporary decenter these and consider things from other points of view.

- What does the situation look like from the new hire's perspective?
- What might they be thinking and feeling, and how might they understand and explain their own behavior?
- Given the context and who they are, what do they believe about you and the other team members?

In terms of deep learning, you might decide to seek understanding with both the author of your algebra textbook, and with a hypothetical student who works through the exercises and comprehends them. You ask similar questions to the ones above, but gear them more towards cognition:

- What is the author assuming I already know how to do here?
- It feels like there's an instruction missing here... from their perspective, why might they have arranged things this way?
- Looking at the kind of practice questions supplied, what is being tested and why did the author feel that was most important?

Step 2: Ideate

In the second step, try to formulate possible answers to the above questions.

Keep it open ended and don't muddy the waters by prematurely coming to conclusions you have no evidence for.

You want to carefully think about what is known and what isn't, what the assumptions are, and how you can start to compare and contrast blind spots.

Perhaps upon reflection you wonder whether the new employee is young and relatively underqualified, and potentially feeling insecure.

This may make them feel they need to prove themselves. If this is so, you can suddenly see their refusal to accept responsibility for the broken equipment: they're mortified!

As for the learning example, you may start to notice that your misunderstanding kicks in at the same step of every worked example. You carefully look at what comes immediately before and after this step. You keep thinking, "it doesn't make sense to do that," but challenge your perspective: "Let's assume it *does* make sense. What would I have to believe in order for me to see it?"

Step 3: Hypothesize

Once you've considered a broad range of alternative views, narrow things down to the best guess (remembering, of course, that these guesses can and should be adjusted in light of new information).

Our hypotheses:

- The new hire is not being difficult on purpose, but may be feeling insecure and unable to ask for help.
- You are missing a crucial detail about an algebraic operation. You suspect there's a coefficient you're not factoring in somewhere.

Now we can test these out.

- If you call the new hire aside and gently, kindly show them the ropes without suggesting that you doubt their competence, does the overall situation in the team improve?
- If you work several algebra problems your way, then compare your solution to the correct solution, can you see a pattern? Is the error the same size every time?

Think through the problem broadly:

- "If my hypothesis is correct, what would I expect to see?"
- "If my hypothesis is incorrect, how would I know?"

Step 4: Observe and Adjust

Let's say you discuss the matter with the new hire in private, then quietly wait and observe what happens over the course of the next week. You notice that they are still a little inept, but have begun to ask for support and guidance when needed, rather than barging ahead to make foolish mistakes.

Hmm.

That's some evidence to support the hypothesis! You decide to gather a little more data.

Let's say also that after your investigation into the algebra problems, you realize that your error is in fact the same every single time—or a multiple of it. You conclude that this is the missing coefficient or constant.

You decide to gather a little more data, keep adjusting your assumptions and stay curious for any fresh insights and revelations. In the algebra example, you may find that this path indirectly leads you to a richer understanding of this concept than you would have had otherwise. You understand this coefficient because, in a very real way, you've just discovered it!

Summary

- **Deep learning of all kinds is associated with verbal fluency,** which tends to be contextual, abstract, precise, and applied meaningfully in everyday life. People with "word consciousness" use language in curious, intentional, adaptable, and novel ways. They interact with words actively and repeatedly.
- The most masterful learners understand **that words are tools.** A "rich" vocabulary isn't necessarily a large or exotic one; it goes beyond definitions, and is about intelligent, contextual application.
- You learn better when you engage multiple parts of your brain simultaneously. **Dual encoding** and

embodied cognition are both ways to make learning **multimodal**. Combining information from two or more different learning channels improve understanding and recall. Strategically combine verbal and nonverbal inputs, enlist your body, and mix up formats and media.

- **Rich, contextual, and embodied learning** is the brain's preference. Movement can be a way to think. Send your brain the same message through two different channels, ears and eyes, then add movement where possible.
- **Perspective-taking is essential for true, deep learning.** Considering the experience of someone other than yourself is not just good for collaboration, conflict resolution, and empathy, but improves cognitive flexibility and insight. Perspective-taking expands your world, broadens understanding and keeps you humble and curious.

Chapter 6: What Memories Are Made Of

Context-Dependent Memory: How Matching the Moment Deepens Your Learning

"It's a poor sort of memory that only works backwards."

- **Lewis Carroll**

Have you ever bumped into someone in the street you instantly recognized, but couldn't really *place*? You knew you knew them, but you couldn't quite recall how or why.

The next day when you're at the corner café and see them working behind the counter, it all comes flooding back to you: they're the barrister! You can now remember who this person is because the first time you encountered them, and every time since then, it's been in the context of this café.

There's a reason for this—human memory is naturally context-dependent.

To put it more precisely, **the creation, storage, and retrieval of memories is heavily influenced by the environment.**

When that person's name and image was first stored in your memory, it was also stored alongside all the relevant contextual information—and this information becomes a vital part of you recalling who they actually are.

Cognitive scientists have long observed that our **recall seems to be better when the retrieval context is the same as the encoding context** (the environment in which we try to remember something closely matches the environment in which we first made that memory).

This phenomenon also explains why we sometimes walk into a room and forget what we're doing, only to remember once we've returned to our previous location.

What's even more fascinating?

It's not just about physical or spatial context, but **emotional context**, for example:

- You get sad and wistful whenever you smell a certain perfume.
- You always get a particular song in your head when driving past a certain landmark in your city.
- You often feel intimidated around architecture that reminds you of your old high school.

Sensory associations arise simply because **most of us don't form memories in a neutral, isolated way, but encode them alongside rich emotional and experiential data.**

We might associate a certain piece of music with the exact shade of coral lipstick of our first choir teacher, or think of titration reactions every time we smell the vaguely "hospital" smell of our old campus chemistry lab...

Sounds, smells, emotions, thought processes, perceptions, tastes, sensations—it's as though your brain takes a rich snapshot of *all* of this at once.

That's good news for us!

The more "handles" we have on a memory, the more we have to grab a hold of when we want to retrieve that memory. Let's learn how.

Recreate the Environment Where You Learned Something

Your brain doesn't store strings of facts. It creates networks—webs of meaning.

The more meaningful you can make an association, the deeper it will be embedded in our memory (Rajaram & Barber, 2008).

When the brain wants to retrieve a certain bit of information, it uses certain cues—words, sensory experiences, emotions.

We can exploit this process by making sure that:

1. The memories we store initially are as meaningfully connected as possible
2. We are providing suitable cues—"handles"—to retrieve that memory

The so-called "reinstatement effect" shows that **when we are in situations that closely mirror the original encoding environment, our recall is better.**

For example:

- You studied chapter 5 while listening to a particular playlist. Later, in the exam, you sing these songs to yourself in your head, making it easier to remember the contents of chapter 5.
- You always do mandolin practice wearing your favorite slippers and sipping a cup of chamomile tea. That means that the taste—or even just the smell—of chamomile tea now helps you remember the pieces you're rehearsing.
- You are revising for an anatomy exam, and recall the birds you watched at the bird feeder outside your window during study sessions. There's just something about recalling the finches and sparrows

that triggers a cascade of memories about anatomy.

The good news is that you don't have to literally duplicate the learning environment—just a cue or two is enough, as is simply *visualizing* that initial learning environment.

Be Mindful of Your Mood and Use It to Your Advantage

It's easy to assume that a calm, neutral state of mind is optimal for memory formation, but this isn't quite true: **emotions act as powerful memory cues** and can trigger both deeper memory encoding and retrieval (Gruneberg et. al., 1994, *Theoretical Aspects of Memory*).

Such "state dependent" or "mood dependent" learning means that we tend to have better recall when our physiological and emotional state closely resembles the one during our initial learning.

So, it's not the emotional state itself that matters—it's the *congruence* of emotional states.

- Were you calm and confident during your studies? You'll remember more during the exam if you help yourself feel that same calmness and confidence.

- Were you energized and alert when you practiced? You'll execute better when you're similarly wired up during a recital or performance.

The best way to ensure that you can duplicate the emotional context of your learning sessions? That's easy—deliberately engineer that emotional context in the first place!

Create a pre-practice and pre-performance ritual. Don't just leave how you feel up to chance. Induce the desired emotional state yourself by running through a deliberate ritual to ground and center yourself in the right headspace. Try:

- A breathing exercise
- A visualization exercise or self-hypnosis
- A physical exercise such as a brisk walk or stretching routine
- A meditation or mindfulness practice
- A prayer or contemplative practice
- Listening to a song that encourages just the right emotional frequency

What about *negative* moods?

Mood dependent memory tends to break down if you are in reactive, fight/flight survival mode. **Fear and negativity narrow your attention span and shut down your ability to encode new memories or retrieve them.**

While it's true that trauma and strong negative experiences can cement certain memories (this is the basis of the re-experiencing that happens during PTSD flashbacks or nightmares), re-experiencing is not the same as genuine recollection and is less about the brain learning anything new and more about it trying to protect itself (Pitts et. al., 2022).

A good mood helps you learn more effectively because it encourages more expansive, connected, and elaborative thinking (Isen, 2008). A good mood makes our cognition more flexible, creative, and hopeful— we're actually prompted to consider the future with optimism and hope.

But what if you're in a bad mood during study or practice?

Don't beat yourself up! You don't have to be ecstatic and ultra-optimistic. But make some gentle moves towards an overall more upbeat frame of mind:

- **Give yourself a small win.** Seek out positive or supportive feedback or tackle a manageable exercise that you can do comfortably, so you feel a little more encouraged and rewarded.
- **Improve your environment.** Could you make small tweaks to your immediate work zone? Don't underestimate the

power of good lighting, a proper chair and adequate ventilation.
- **Seek novelty.** A bad mood may just be a sign that you need to change things up or try something new. Fire up your creativity or do something unexpected. When we're in a bad mood, our thinking can become rigid and rule-based (Schwabe, 2012); escape this by deliberately allowing yourself to break the rules a little, play and have fun.
- **Build hope.** You may feel down just because you've lost sight of the end point. Remind yourself of what you're doing and why. Visualize the finish line.

Use Contextual Cues to Trigger Future Actions and Recall

Memories are not just about the past.

They're about the present, and how we plan for the future.

In short, our memory is like an organizing thread that helps us to pull together life's disparate experiences into a coherent whole—past, present, and future. And context is a big part of how that thread works.

Prospective memory = remembering to remember.

Like Lew Carroll says, it's a poor sort of memory that only works backwards! Prospective memory helps us work it *forwards*.

We don't just have to passively sit and wait for memories to arrive, we can proactively encourage ourselves to remember. Take a look at the following examples:

- "The moment I open that exam paper I'm going to quickly jot down the seven main points I've studied."
- "When I hear those opening bars of *Cello Concerto in G Major*, I'll immediately try to remember that trick with my hand placement."
- "When it's 5 PM, I run through my ten vocabulary words for the day, whether I'm walking home or taking the bus that day."

The more we can deliberately connect certain ideas or memories with specific environmental cues, the more we can take charge of our future memory... right now in the present (Einstein et. al., 2005).

As above, your cues can be based on:

- actions/events
- times
- places

These things act as triggers—they remind you to remember. This way, your cues become embedded in natural, everyday contexts. Essentially, you are leaving sticky notes in your environment to help you recall important information—but in this case the sticky notes are not visual and material, but contextual and situational.

To sum up—context-dependent memory is always superior, whether "context" means

- the learning environment
- the state (emotion) during learning
- the various contextual cues and triggers

Emotion Tagging: Enhance Memory With Mini Stories

"Storytelling is the most powerful way to put ideas into the world today."

- **Robert McAfee Brown**

Storytelling is not just a good way to put ideas into the world; it's a good way to embed ideas into *our own minds*… and keep them there.

When police interview an eyewitness, they routinely encourage a recounting of "just the facts." In a court of law, witnesses are told to relay information, not necessarily their interpretation of that information.

And yet, for human beings, emotion isn't an impediment to memory—it's one of the ways we get memories to stick in the first place.

Facts are easy to forget—but stories tend to stick. That's because stories do more than deliver dry information; they activate the **emotional centers of the brain**, making ideas more vivid, meaningful, and easier to remember.

Emotion tagging is deliberately imbuing narratives with emotion in order to make those narratives easier to recall.

- Curiosity
- Empathy
- Surprise
- Disgust
- Wonder

When stories appeal to us emotionally, they instantly become more relatable, more meaningful, more human. If we feel a certain way about a certain piece of information, we suddenly *care* a whole lot more—and we are infinitely more inclined to remember those things that we care about!

The emotional significance of a piece of data can change how well we remember that data.

Reverse engineer it: If we wish to remember a piece of data well, we can deliberately attach emotional significance to it. This creates stronger, more enduring memories and can even reduce the perceived cognitive load of recall. Here's how:

Step 1: Emotional arousal triggers activity in the amygdala.

Step 2: The amygdala modulates the activity of other parts of the brain, such as the hippocampus. It can down- or up-regulate synaptic plasticity; i.e., determine the strength of neural connections and ultimately the formation of memories.

Step 3: Emotional arousal, mediated through the amygdala, then acts as a tag on a certain memory that tells the brain "This is important." The brain is more likely to cement these things as long-term memories.

To put it simply, the involvement of the amygdala (often called an "emotional center" of the brain) triggers a stronger memory formation process (Richter-Levin & Akirav, 2003).

When emotion is involved, the brain pays closer attention and forms deeper and richer connections... which means that it holds onto information for longer.

Whatever it is you're trying to better recall, emotion is the secret-sauce to making memory stick. Here are three ways to use this emotion in everyday learning.

Create a Short "Micro-Narrative" for Each Concept

According to Gal Richter-Levin, a professor of behavioral neuroscientist and one of the main proponents of the theory of emotion tagging:

> "At any given moment our brain is bombarded with stimuli from our external and internal environment. Within this flood of information, effective memory systems, such as the hippocampus, are required to be able to identify the more relevant aspects, in order to transfer only those to longer-term memory. The emotional implication of stimuli was suggested as important cues for their significance, which should promote their consolidation. We termed this concept—'Emotional Tagging.'"

One of the amygdala's main jobs is to make sense of a complex and chaotic world of stimuli. It looks out at the environment and essentially asks the question:

"What matters here?"

To take it further, this is really another question in disguise:

"Why should I care? What does this have to do with me?"

One of the best ways to truly help your brain grasp and retain new information is to make it matter, on an emotional level.

A narrative is not just entertainment—it's a data container. It's an informational format that tells us what matters and is "part of the story"—and what is irrelevant and can be ignored. We are usually invested in only those parts of a story that relate directly to the narrative drive, to the characters involved, or to the emotional stakes—which we can identify with because we, too, feel those emotions.

How can we apply this to our own deep learning practice?

It's not necessary to turn everything into an epic saga; a one-minute story or a quick tale of a few sentences is all it takes to activate the amygdala and get us paying attention. For example:

- Instead learning about the four different chemical bases in a DNA molecule, make each of them *characters*—let's say two married couples. Create a quick backstory that explains their attributes and make the story drama-filled.

- Whenever you encounter a new historical character, central theorist or key contributor in your area of study, form a personal opinion about them. Relate them to people in your own life. Find colorful details—real or imagined—that bring this person and their contribution to life.
- Connect data points using narrative. Turn cause-effect relationships or processes into stories with a hero, antagonist, plot arc, and resolution. "One day, a single lonely oxygen atom was walking down the road when he encountered his old friend, the methane molecule…"

Use Emotional Analogies That Make Sense to You

Remember that the amygdala's job is to scan a complex and rich environment and filter out everything that is relevant. How does it decide what's relevant?

Well that depends—quite literally—on YOU.

Your brain will always pay preferential attention to anything that is connected to your goals, your desires, and your survival. To make new material stick, then, try connecting everything you encounter to yourself in some way.

This takes abstract concepts and makes them a part of your own world—something you will naturally pay more attention to and recall in greater detail.

- **Studying risk-taking in entrepreneurship?** Think about the last time you took a calculated risk in your own personal life.
- **Revising a complicated economic concept?** Create an analogy or metaphor that speaks to you—perhaps using the value and rarity of an item you collect, a game you play, or a purchase you've made.
- **Learning about marketing?** Compare certain concepts to texting someone you like and waiting for a reply.

Sometimes, you may have to make a little effort to convert new material into a story you genuinely care about. However, this is germane load—it's effort that will pay off.

Remember that the stories you tell and the emotion tags you add are all private and meant to appeal to nobody else but you. It doesn't matter if it doesn't really "make sense"—if it fits in your world emotionally, then go for it.

Masterful learners have known for years that the details people almost never seem to forget are those that are:

- Shocking, unexpected, or surprising
- A little rude or scandalous
- Totally outrageous
- Funny or silly
- Really bizarre and weird
- Arresting and striking

When creating mnemonics, mind maps, or mental shortcuts, remember this. **The more outlandish the cue, the more your amygdala is involved, and the better your memory.** A naughty rhyme or mental picture may *feel* juvenile… but you certainly won't forget it!

When you *feel* something, your brain remembers it better. When something seems like it's a meaningful and relevant part of your unique life, it suddenly doesn't feel like abstract material at all, but simply part of your world.

Make it Personal with Your Own Examples

Recall that memories are not dry strings of facts, but networks of meaningfully connected information.

You can strengthen your recall by consistently finding out how to incorporate new information into your existing memory banks. One of the best ways to wire in new ideas is via emotion.

After encountering some new information, pause and ask:

- "Have I ever experienced this or something like this?"
- "Does this remind me of something in my own life?"
- "How does this idea or concept apply to my own problems?"
- "Can I find an example of this in my life right now?"

Asking these questions anchors new material into old memory webs. Importantly, you're doing this **not just with logic, but with emotion.**

Now, it may seem kind of hard to turn some study material into a personal story. Can we really relate our everyday lives to computer programming, ancient history, pure math, or a foreign language?

The answer is *yes*—and the harder you work to find the links and connections, the more helpful they are likely to be.

Ask your mind to deliberately seek out details that you can connect with or generate examples so that you can bring the concept to life in your own experience.

For example:

- As you learn a new coding concept, immediately think of how you would personally use it in your life and work—be as specific as possible.
- As you learn more about certain historical events, try to see how it connects to your own ancestry. You may even invent a great-great-great-great-grandfather figure and try to imagine the events through his eyes!
- Pure math might seem as abstract as you can get, but remember, you are not trying to find logical connections to the material, but emotional ones. It may sound silly, but humorous memes, "context-dependent" memory techniques and leaning into the human aspects of your learning process will make even the most abstract mathematical concept seem more relatable.
- A foreign language may seem rather remote and inaccessible until you become emotionally invested in a soap opera in that language.
- As a last resort, you can even create more lasting tags on new information by zooming in on what you *disagree* with or *dislike*. Sounds counterintuitive but one way to make sure you don't forget certain

concepts is to continually imagine yourself arguing against them!

Bringing emotion and narrative into your studies isn't cheating—it's exactly how your brain learns best.

Emotion-laden stories force us to engage more deeply, to pay attention, to interact with what we're encountering, and to tie it more firmly into our existing knowledge. **Deep work can be emotional, human, and personal.**

Conflict-Based Encoding: Strengthen Learning by Challenging Misconceptions

"You must never feel badly about making mistakes... as long as you take the trouble to learn from them. For you often learn more by being wrong for the right reasons than you do by being right for the wrong reasons."

- **Norton Juster**

In the previous chapter, we touched on something interesting and unintuitive: A little friction and opposition can actually enhance memory.

We tend to remember those moments when:

- We found out we were wrong about something
- We were totally surprised by something
- We discovered a weird incongruence that really gave us pause

Conflict-based encoding is a powerful learning strategy that involves **intentionally introducing an element of confusion, error, misconception, or conflict.**

It's not just about better recall, but deeper understanding overall.

The idea is that you:

- Deliberately introduce a conflict
- Intentionally create a moment of tension or confusion
- *Then* you introduce the correct answer

Why? What could be the benefit of deliberate confusion?

Your brain is constantly trying to reduce uncertainty, answer questions, and figure out what are signals and what is noise.

When you introduce a little moment of strangeness or conflict, you immediately tell your brain to:

- Pause
- Pay very close attention

- Be on the lookout for the *right* answer; i.e., be receptive to correction

Slow, deliberate attention and curiosity? That's a *supremely* conducive state of mind for deep work!

Conflict-based encoding uses *contrast* and the *unexpected* to heighten awareness and trigger an active engagement in resolving tension.

Mistakes are learning fuel.

A "correction" is always more memorable than something that is already "correct" to start with.

And surprise is the royal road to emotion-based encoding!

Our brain remembers a mistake-then-correction better than it remembers a correct answer presented upfront with no tension. The result is more durable memories that your own brain has played a role in creating.

Typically, this learning method is utilized by teachers deliberately structuring prompts and learning materials to maximize engagement. A teacher might, for example:

- Offer a false but plausible statement
- Have the student try to figure it out
- Eventually correct them

This way, the path to the correct statement becomes that much clearer in the student's mind. They have seen for themselves that the wrong approach doesn't work. The right approach is then not something they're simply handed by the teacher, but something they actively reason their way toward.

Instead of avoiding mistakes, they are deliberately used to pattern deeper understanding. Knowing what you now know about narratives, emotion, and perspective-taking, you can also see why this approach might be so effective.

Whether you are self-learning topics in science, history, or business, or just trying to unlearn bad habits and biases, conflict-based encoding can help. Below are some ideas.

Challenge What You Think You Know

If you are self-learning and in the role of your own teacher, you will need to carefully consider how to introduce generative conflict into your own study journey.

One great way: Start with what you think you already know.

Is there something you currently accept without question? Think about all the things that "everyone knows" or that you've automatically taken as true——*are* they true? How do you know?

Importantly, you ask these questions for two separate reasons:

1. To actually discover the correct answer.
2. To more firmly cement that answer in your mind once you find it.

What happens when you ask the question, set out to try and find the answer, and then discover a mismatch between what you thought the facts were, and what they actually are?

The "conflict" itself heightens your awareness, attention, and learning. **Discovering an error is memorable.**

For example, you may be working through an online psychology course and hear a fellow student casually mention, "Humans only use 10% of their brains."

You realize that this idea is something that you've passively believed in yourself, even though you don't know why, or whether you should.

So, you go off to find out.

To cut to the chase, this "fact" isn't a fact at all, but a fascinating cultural artifact arising from misrepresentations of early neuroscientific research. These half-truths were turbo-charged by popular self-help and science fiction, so that now everyone "knows" that you only use a tiny portion of your brain, and who knows what you could do if you "unlocked" the rest...

The interesting thing here is that by digging around to find the truth, you learn so much more, and in a much more engaged way, about all sorts of interesting topics in the history of psychology.

Caveat 1: This method only works if you can sincerely challenge yourself and drop ideas you have no evidence for. Doubling down is great for the ego, but terrible for deep learning.

Caveat 2: If you find out you were right after all? Great. It's never "for nothing" to confirm something for yourself, because now your knowledge is real and hard won, not second-hand.

Reflect on Your Mistakes to Learn Smarter

The natural human tendency is to avoid mistakes and errors, and if we must face them, we like to make the encounter as quick and painless as possible, right? You'll recognize this as part of the fixed mindset.

However, what would your learning process look like if you celebrated every time a mistake naturally arose in your world?

Once you realize you've made a mistake, bought into a misconception, or misunderstood something, don't just try to hurry on and forget about it. Yes, there is value in swiftly moving on to the "correct" thing, but there is also value in *reflecting on your mistake.*

When you mess up, pause and pay attention.

Celebrate!

A mistake is not only evidence of growth and learning, but a potential opportunity for further growth and learning, depending on how you play it.

Ask yourself:

- "Why did I think that was true?"
- "What exactly led me to make that mistake?"
- "What's missing in my understanding for me to have made that error?"
- "What assumption does this misunderstanding come from?"

You want to uncover the right path.

You want to make sure that you're not making the same mistake again.

But you also want to shine a mental spotlight on this moment in particular, because that spotlight will help reinforce the correct approach in your long-term memory.

Your knowledge becomes clearer, stronger, and more self-determined. You take charge of your learning process. Engaging with a "silly mistake" often reveals deeper misconceptions that can improve your comprehension of a wide range of ideas you never even knew were connected.

For example, one day you realize with some embarrassment that a "test tube baby" is not in fact grown start to finish in a test tube. But when you start reflecting on this error, you realize that it shows a huge knowledge gap around not just the IVF process, but about human reproduction in general.

Adopt a growth mindset.

Being confused, mistaken, or misinformed? That's nothing to be ashamed of. But from that point you have a choice:

- Try to conceal, deny, or avoid the mistake
- Allow the mistake to teach you something useful

Only one approach yields any gain and leads to deep learning!

Summary

- The creation, storage, and retrieval of memories is heavily influenced by the environment; leverage this by **making new memories deliberately context-dependent**. Recall improves when the retrieval context is the same as the encoding context.

- Emotional and experiential associations matter too; the brain doesn't store strings of neutral facts but connected webs of meaning. Replicate learning environments and deliberately create and call on relevant cues——emotions being a primary cue. Create a pre-practice and pre-performance ritual to proactively use your mood to your advantage.
- Make use of **prospective memory** by using conscious reminders and contextual, embedded cues to help yourself remember things in future.
- Enhance your memory by using **narrative**, which is more vivid and memorable than dry fact. **Emotion tagging** is deliberately imbuing narratives with emotion in order to make those narratives easier to recall. Make stories personal and use emotion-laden analogies and associations to cement encoding. When you *feel* something, your brain remembers it better.
- **Conflict-based encoding** tells us that corrected mistakes and misconceptions are more easily remembered. **Mistakes are learning fuel**. We learn by challenging assumptions and reflecting on the mistakes we make, even if those mistakes are deliberate!

Conclusion

"The world is a university and everyone in it is a teacher. Make sure when you wake up in the morning, you go to school."

- **T. D. Jakes**

No matter your innate intelligence or skill level, and regardless of your personal obstacles or limitations, you *can* become a master of deep, adaptive, and deliberate learning.

Energy and focus are limited, and there will always be more things to learn than time to learn them! Yet with a proactive approach and the right mindset, you will always get the most out of every hour, *every minute,* that you spend in study or practice.

Let's recap:

- The most impactful overall change you can make is upgrading from a fixed mindset to a **growth mindset**. Expect effort, make friends with failure, and embrace process, not outcome.

- From now on, think of yourself as an **autotelic** personality. You are no longer mindlessly chasing quantity; instead you are driven from within by value, purpose, meaning, and quality.
- Think in levels. **Metacognition** and deliberate practice are the key to intelligent, purposeful activity. It's not about tools, tricks, and hacks, but **strategy**. Learning is problem solving. Make it a dialogue.
- Instead of being passive and reactive, commit to **curiosity**, **meaningful questioning,** and **active engagement**. Become your own teacher. Author your own curriculum. And whatever you do, don't camp out indefinitely in your comfort zone!
- Whatever your goals, work on your language skills—including **multimodal fluency**; i.e.. plasticity in both perspective and format. Mix it up—verbal, nonverbal, all five senses, and your physical body, too! Cognitive flexibility means smoothly translating from one mode to another.
- Forgo rote memorization; instead opt for **context-, emotion-, and conflict-dependent learning.** To remember something, make it real and emotional. Make it matter.

Practically speaking, the good news is that so much of what you've been taught at school is simply not necessary.

You have permission to permanently forget about:

- Mindless re-reading
- Highlighting
- Underlining
- "Going over" long form notes
- Cramming
- Rote memorization

Instead, focus on the handful of study methods that are proven to work, time and again:

- Instructional scaffolding
- Spaced repetition or distributed practice
- Interleaving
- Gamifying
- Managing cognitive load
- Managing stress levels
- Prediction and pre-testing
- Teaching yourself or others
- Multimodal learning and dual coding
- Perspective-taking
- Context-dependent memory
- Emotion tagging
- Conflict-based encoding

Becoming a masterful learner is all about the daily choices and decisions you make.

Consistency beats dramatic overnight transformations.

Variety and **adaptability** win over mindless repetition every time.

Choose always to focus on just one thing at a time, do a little every day, and do it as well as you can. Pay attention, be honest about your performance, learn what you can, adjust, and try again. Repeat, forever.

Be active, not passive. Take responsibility for your learning process and never lose hope—failure will always be one of your best teachers, and if you're lucky, it will be a faithful and constant companion.

Finally, remind yourself that time spent learning never goes to waste. **Learning is a life's work, and a true education never comes to an end.**

www.ingramcontent.com/pod-product-compliance
Lightning Source LLC
Chambersburg PA
CBHW060558080526
44585CB00013B/605